TARA MILLS

CHAKRAS FOR BEGINNERS

A Comprehensive Guide to Balancing Your Energy Centers
(2023)

Contents

CHAPTER 1: CROWN CHAKRA

Our emotions are physically present in our bodies. On a fundamental level, our bodies communicate with the energies around us, and distinct lively motivations are often tied to a specific piece of the body and chakra that is debilitated or unbalanced.

Each chakra represents a significant life practice or challenge that may help us get a better understanding of our own and otherworldly forces. This encourages us to find out how to conquer obstacles, let go of energetic barriers, and tread the path to spiritual consciousness.

"There is a sanctuary, a hallowed place, a mosque, a congregation where I bow in my spirit." Rabia al-Basri

This chapter examines the Crown (or seventh) Chakra from the inside out, looking at its emotional and mental connections to the physical world.

The seventh and highest chakra links us to the divine and deep nature. It also considers otherworldliness in order to fit into our everyday existence. The Crown Chakra, also known as Sahasrara, is straightforwardly altered to seek a deep connection with the cosmos. It is the petition's chakra.

We know that the Root Chakra functions as a cellar or reusing center that exempts the gathering of energy that it no longer requires. The Crown Chakra serves as a repository for the energy we acquire via good thoughts, actions, and shows of trust, introspection, and prayer. It is here that we might soar beyond the components of life and cooperate with "God."

Crown Chakra Essential Qualities:

In terms of the physical body, the Crown Chakra is the conduit for human life force, which flows inexhaustibly into the body's vitality framework from the greater cosmos (God or the Tao). This power nourishes the body, brain, and soul, and it spreads vitality throughout the physical body and down the lower chakras.

This is why activating Kundalini vitality and the Sushumna, Ida, and Pingala (the body's basic requirements or vitality pathways) are so important. It doesn't merely allow energy to rise from the bottom. However, it also allows Crown Chakra energy to freely flow throughout the body and into the lower chakras.

Connection: The Crown Chakra

The seventh chakra affects the major bodily frameworks: the central anxious, solid, and skin. Along these lines, skin disorders like rashes, skin irritation, or dermatitis may indicate that your Crown Chakra is in disamicability.

The Crown Chakra generates enthusiasm, persuasive and prophetic ideas, magical connections, and supernatural notions. Are you experiencing strange dreams lately?

Your Crown Chakra might be communicating with you.

The Crown Chakra represents energy:

The Sahasrara, as an emblem, holds the ideal sort of prana (living energy) and revolves around the region of supernatural quality.

As a result, persons who have a blocked Sahasrara are biased and unable to understand the master plan, and they need inspiration and condemnation from others for their urgency or stagnation. They, too, have a skewed perspective on life, death, and otherworldliness.

The Crown Chakra teaches us that at certain points in our lives, we must let an old stage "kick the bucket" in order to be regenerated once more.

Humanness is the Crown Chakra:

This is the chakra of humanity. Here, we know we are all right now, and that all of our souls have come to experience what it is like to be in a human body. Individuals who can't interact with others or have a receptive outlook and, for the most part, experience the negative effects of issues identified with sympathy on a global scale are isolated and generally hostile to faith and spirituality.

What Does the Crown Chakra Teach Us?

The vibrancy of the Sahasrara encourages us to seek a more meaningful relationship with the heavenly in everything that we do. This is why you hear experts, yogis, and designers say they had a supernatural contact that motivated them throughout their training, or maybe of individuals who had a joyous discovery that provided them insight into an outstanding notion.

Individuals must not destroy the seventh chakra's specific otherworldly relationship with religion. Religion is founded in groups, implying that we are safe in numbers. Otherworldliness is a one-of-a-kind experience aimed at dispelling worries of the physical world, associating with the divine, and comprehending the amazing resides inside each of us.

The seventh chakra is also known as:
- The crown chakra
- Sahasrara
- Shunya
- Niralambapuri

The Sanskrit word **"Sahasrara"** is sometimes used to refer to the seventh chakra. It
is often understood as "thousand petals."

<u>Shading of the Crown Chakra:</u>

The head chakra is often articulated with white shading.

However, it can also be described as deep purple. The auric color of crown chakra energy may also be gold, white, or dazzling light.

<u>Image of the Crown Chakra:</u>

The Crown Chakra picture is composed of:

1. A ring
2. a million petals

The dominant color in the crown chakra picture is white. Its petals are multicolored, like a rainbow. The circle is often contrasted with a picture of a full moon.

Make every cell in your body shiver and rejoice!

The majority of us have robust squares and awkward nature, as well as vitality-destroying propensities, which prohibit us from reaching our maximum imperativeness, causing us to feel drained, scattered, dull… even ill.

<u>Area of the Crown Chakra:</u>

The seventh chakra is most often associated with the highest point of the head or somewhat above the head. It sits like a crown, radiating upwards, thus the name "The Crown Chakra." It is associated with the pituitary organ, as well as the pineal and nerve centers. The pituitary organ and the nerve center collaborate to govern the endocrine framework. Because of its location, the crown chakra is inextricably linked to the cerebrum and the whole sensory system.

It is worth noting that the seventh chakra has a strong connection with the first chakra since the two are located at opposite ends of the chakra framework.

Crown Chakra's Social Aspects:

The Crown Chakra is associated with the following mental and social characteristics:

- Cognizance
- familiarity with greater consciousness, astuteness in what is sacred
- Association with the ephemeral,
- Unrestricted acknowledgment, freedom from limiting examples
- Fellowship with higher levels of consciousness via pleasure and joy
- Nearness

The crown chakra is associated with the magnitude of our restrictions, whether they be near home or tied to existence.

It is here that the Catch-22 becomes a norm where opposite extremes are one. In general, the quality of awareness that supports the head chakra is amazing.

We experience a state of blissful connection with everything that is of otherworldly ecstasy when we are soaked in the energy of the head chakra.

This chakra provides access to the greatest levels of clarity and enlightenment.

This chakra is seen by some as the gateway to the grandiose self or the heavenly self to all-inclusive consciousness. It is linked to the infinite and ubiquitous.

Imbalance in the Crown Chakra:

When the Crown Chakra is out of balance, it might manifest as separation from the soul and persistent skepticism about what is sanctified.

An overactive head chakra, on the other hand, may manifest as dissociation from the body. Living in your head, being disconnected from your body and natural concerns, excessive attachment to serious topics, and closed-mindedness are all symptoms of living in your head.

The Crown Chakra's Power:

The more people can connect with the intensity of this chakra, the more it will shift our collective consciousness for a massive scope toward a more all-encompassing grasp of wellness, disease, the planet, biodiversity, and humanity in general.

The goal of this natural strategy is to rise beyond every illusion and discover the inherent intensity of the soul. We recognize that we are accountable for what we create and must so find out how to behave, think, and speak with devotion and wisdom throughout our lives.

Remember that the only dreams to profit from are all physical and enthusiastic deterrents. Always look for the importance of each situation, follow it, and then let it go when it's no longer relevant.

Methods for Crown Chakra Healing:

Close your eyes and accept that you are the cosmos and that the universe is you. All of the incredible courses' limitless brilliance is coursing through and inside you.

1. Crown Chakra Yoga Asanas: Headstand, Crane Pose, Shoulder Stand
2. Crown Chakra Gems: Celestine, Blue Sapphire, and Clear Quartz
3. Crown Chakra fragrance treatment: Ylang, Rosewood, and Lotus of the Water Lily

We are our own congregation, church, synagogue, or mosque, and we should just shut our eyes and take in the vibrancy of the amazing all around us and flow through our chakras. It is the beginning of our ability and the vitality that drives our science.

We have no option but to live a meaningful life once we realize the substance of which we are constituted.

CHAPTER 2: THE THIRD EYE CHAKRA

The sixth chakra is also known as:
- The third eye chakra.
- The chakra of the temple
- Chakra Ajna
- Dvidak Padma
- Bhru Madhya

The most well-known Sanskrit word for the Third Eye chakra is "Ajna," which means "order" and "seeing."

This chakra is associated with the **"preeminent component,"** which is the combination of a significant number of components in their natural structure.

Third Eye Chakra's Yogic Importance:

The third eye, or Ajna chakra, in yogic mysticism, is where we transcend beyond duality - the duality of an individual "I" apart from the rest of the universe, of a character that exists independently of everything else.

"A yogi who has passed through the Vishuddha Chakra at the throat to the Ajna Chakra rises above the five components and becomes liberated (Mukta) from the subjugation of time-bound awareness," writes Harish Johari. This is where I-cognizance is absorbed into super-awareness." Chakras: Energy Centers of Transformation (Harish Johari).

Shading of the Third Eye Chakra:
The third eye chakra is usually associated with the color purple or a shade of

blue-purple. The auric color of third eye chakra vigor may also be described as transparent purple or somewhat blue-white.

Make every cell in your body shiver and rejoice!

The majority of us have lively squares and uneven personalities, as well as vitality-assaulting propensities that restrict us from reaching our maximum potential, causing us to feel exhausted, scattered, bored, and even ill.

In contrast to its shade, it is distinguished by the nature of its iridescence or delicate brightness, which reminds us of moonlight.

Image of the Third Eye Chakra:

The depiction of the Third Eye chakra has two components that are often associated with astuteness:

1. The perplexing triangle
2. The lotus flower

Area of the Third Eye Chakra:

The most often recognized location for the 6th chakra is between the brows, just above the bridge of your nose. In contrast to popular belief, it is located between the eyes, where the brows meet, rather than in the temple.

It may also be portrayed as being in the cranium behind the eyes. Although the optional chakras run along the midline of the temple, the third eye chakra is frequently found lower down.

The third eye chakra is similar to the pineal organ, which controls biorhythms such as sleep and wake time. It is a mental organ that is a focus of attention due to its association with the recognition and influence of light and altered or "mysterious" states of awareness. It is located near the optical nerves and, as such, is sensitive to visual stimuli and changes in illumination.

Third Eye Chakra Attributes of Conduct:

The third eye chakra corresponds to the mental and conducts characteristics. The following are the main characteristics of the Third Eye Chakra:

The sixth chakra, also known as the frontal chakra, the Third Eye chakra, the internal eye, or "Ajna" in Sanskrit, is concerned with our psychological faculties, mental aptitudes, and how we evaluate beliefs and viewpoints.

The psyche chakra is located between our eyes and is actually related to the cerebrum, pituitary, and pineal organs. It resonates with our mind's vigor, just as our conscious and unconscious mental impulses do.

Intuitive Third Eye Chakra:

This is the chakra of intuition, astuteness, and instinct. It is known as our 'third eye' and the otherworldly focus in Eastern techniques of thinking, which connects with the sane brain to enhance our inherent comprehension to see beyond the veil of deceit known as "Maya."

An Unblocked Mind is the Third Eye Chakra:

The 6th chakra's overall obstacles include unlocking the brain and distinguishing between contemplations prompted by quality, fear, and fantasy. It is learning how to construct a general mentality and retreating from bodily and mental hallucinations. We may transcend beyond our worries, concerns, and fears to really know our souls from the inside.

The third eye contains a unique combination of facts, anxieties, individual experiences, and memories that are always active inside the vitality of the psychological body.

Truth is represented by the Third Eye Chakra:

The focus of this chakra is decoding what we consider to be true and what is clear. A negative memory can occasionally show up as truth to an individual later on. For example, if an individual is made to accept, they are fat or terrible their entire life, this can show up as certainty inside their idea designs and thus, they will create body dysmorphia and low confidence.

The Third Eye Chakra is a source of wisdom:

The iconography of the Third Eye Chakra secures previous deception and our self-caused recognitions. It is separating generalizations, seeing through media figments, and achieving detachment from true cultural forces.

The Third Eye Chakra's intensity sees your chance beyond the realms of sensible imagination.' Nothing is really holding you back - it is only your brain that has influence over you, and if you can master the psyche, you will be able to overcome any limitations.

The third eye chakra serves as a tool for seeing the less obvious aspects of reality. It confines physical abilities to the realm of inconspicuous energy. Awakening your third eye allows you to become more receptive to instinctual reasonableness and inside awareness.

Because it connects us to a different way of seeing, the third eye chakra's images are frequently difficult to describe verbally. It brings us even closer to the unspeakable and the elusive. Third-eye dreams are typically less noticeable than regular dreams: they may be misty, phantomlike, clouded, or dream-like. In rare situations, though, the interior dreams may be as obvious as a film playing before your eyes.

Supporting awareness of third eye chakra vitality may need a center and the ability to relax into a different way of perceiving. When we center our brain and awareness, we can see past the interruptions and deceptions that remain in front of us and have more understanding to live and be more profoundly aligned with our most noteworthy great. Vision is one of the third eye's many characteristics.

The third eye chakra, like the world of spirits, is analogous to model measurements.

Third Eye Chakra Imbalance:

When the Third Eye Chakra is out of balance, it may manifest as:

•Feeling trapped in your daily routine without the ability to examine your previous troubles and create a guiding vision for yourself.

•Overactive third chakra without assistance from the rest of the chakra system may manifest as dreams that seem more authentic than reality, guilty pleasure in mystic dreams, and figments.

•Not being able to set up a dream for oneself and acknowledge it, dismissing everything profound or beyond the ordinary, and not being able to see the bigger picture.

•There is a lack of clarity.

Our emotions are physically present in our bodies. On a subtle level, our bodies communicate with the energies around us, and particular lively driving factors, for the most part, genuinely correspond legitimately to a specific piece of the body and chakra that is debilitated or unbalanced.

Each chakra represents a significant life practice or challenge that may help us get a more holistic understanding of our own and otherworldly forces. As a result, we are encouraged to find out how to overcome obstacles, let go of enthusiastic impediments, and travel the path toward abstract consciousness.

"Believe in your instincts. Your mistakes should be your own, not someone else's." - Billy Wilder

This chapter investigates the Third Eye (or 6th) chakra's enthusiastic and mental relationship with the physical universe from top to bottom.

What Do the Chakras of the Third Eye Teach Us?

The sixth chakra helps us to recognize that no one person or social gathering has the power to direct our lives. When change is noticeable, it is a direct outcome of a larger karmic dynamic or chain of events that has driven you and is propelling you forward into the next chapter of your life.

For example, it may appear that someone has manipulated you into believing you should continue in a job you despise; however, their thoughts are only a figment of how you should live and will hold you, hostage, for a lifetime and can even be conveyed into further rebirths as a karmic exercise you must absorb and develop from.

The Third Eye Chakra's Power:

The Third Eye Chakra teaches us that death is nothing to be afraid of; it is important to appreciate your time on this earth since everything you do after that is to depart your body. Nonetheless, death serves as a portal into the subsequent exercise of presence.

Similarly, as we are made great in the world, we can leave this natural domain whole. We are not meant to die in pain or illness. In essence, they are karmic indicators that we have created for ourselves. The conscious brain may evolve and separate from anguish, allowing the soul to be released from the body without enduring agony, and this choice is available to everyone.

Indications of Third Eye Chakra Imbalance:

The basic problem with this chakra is an unwillingness to look within and confront our fears. In certain circumstances, we hate realizing the truth, which causes our minds to become jumbled; we dread analysis and other people's thoughts about us, and we dread our shadow side and its qualities.

A fair 6th chakra has a great awareness of growth and change, understanding that there is a time for ends as well as beginnings. It can release old thought examples and grab the new—for those who can't keep fearing the unknown and hence despise life.

Our thoughts and mentalities have a significant role in determining or destroying the strength of our bodies. Despondency, for example, directly inhibits our immune framework and affects our own cells from recovering since the body communicates with the brain.

Our mending technique is hampered by negative deductions such as indignation, sharpness, want, and scorn. Recuperation necessitates brain, heart, and body unity, as well as the awareness that the physical world, including our bodies, serves as an educator.

If this chakra becomes blocked, it may cause insomnia, headaches, terrible nightmares, intense sadness, and otherworldly egotism.

Third Eye Chakra Healing Instructions:

Consider and cooperate with the truth inside your spirit, recognize any self-limiting beliefs, and be in touch with your interior orientation.

1. Third Eye Chakra Yoga Poses: Downward Dog, Plow Pose, and Lotus Pose
2. Third Eye Chakra Precious Stones: Lapis Lazuli, Labradorite, and Opal
3. Treatment based on a fragrance to activate the Third Eye Chakra: Frankincense, Basil, and Almond Blossom

We get mental clarity when we totally interact with the power from inside the Ajna. We can look beyond the brain and all of its desires, longings, tensions, worries, and judgments. At that time, we enter the realms of information, consciousness, and instinct.

In Eastern spiritual scriptures, the Third Eye Chakra is referred to as the expanse of nectar. Is it correct to suggest that you are willing to swim your vast sea to reach a state of illumination?

CHAPTER 3: THROAT CHAKRA

The fifth chakra is referred to as:
- The throat chakra.
- Vishuddha
- Padma Kanth
- Shodash Dala

The most well-known Sanskrit word for the Throat chakra is "Vishudda," which means "pure" or "decontaminated."

This chakra is associated with the element of sound. The sound is sent into the air through the throat, and its vibration may be felt in our ears as well as throughout our bodies. It is an essential tool for correspondence and articulation.

Shading of the Throat Chakra:

The Throat chakra is often associated with the color's blue turquoise or marine green/blue. The auric color of throat chakra vigor may also be described as a smokey purple or turquoise.

Image of the Throat Chakra:

The Throat chakra picture is composed of:

1. A sixteen-petalled hover
2. A bow with a hover in it

It is sometimes represented as a circle with a downward-pointing triangle inside which is etched into another circle.

The petals are either smoky purple or greyish lavender in color.

Make every cell in your body shiver and rejoice!

Many of us have fiery squares and irregular features, as well as energy-disturbing proclivities that restrict us from reaching our full potential, causing us to feel tired, dispersed, dull... even ill.

Fifth Chakra Zone:

The fifth chakra is most often associated with the degree of the neck. Remember that this chakra is multidimensional and is commonly described as leaving the front of the neck and moving inward with a little upward edge.

The Throat chakra is involved with the mouth, jaws, tongue, pharynx, and sensation of taste and is tied to the pharyngeal and brachial plexus. It's also related to the shoulders and the neck.

The thyroid is an organ associated with the fifth chakra because it governs the preparation of vitality in the body via temperature, development, and, in large part, digestion.

Throat Chakra Social Attributes:

The Throat Chakra is associated with the following Mental and Social Attributes:

- Articulation is the ability to express yourself clearly and stand up.
- Correspondence, whether spoken or nonverbal, external or internal.
- Association with the etheric sphere, the less visible areas of the soul, and innate talents.
- The proclivity to create and predict ideas and plans in the actual world, knowing

your cause for working.

- A fantastic sense of timing.

Your Throat Chakra is for declaring yourself: your truth, reason in daily life, and innovativeness. Take note that this chakra has a trait with the second chakra or sacral chakra, which is the center of emotions and imagination. The throat chakra focuses on conveying and anticipating innovation into the globe in accordance with its ideal structure or genuineness.

Another function of the throat chakra is to connect you to your soul. Because of its location, it is commonly referred to as the "bottleneck" of vitality growth in the body. It is located not far from the higher chakras of the head. Opening the throat chakra will help you adapt your vision to the actual world and release pressure that may be affecting the heart chakra, which is located close to underneath.

The throat chakra is linked to the etheric body, which is claimed to store the blueprint or ideal arrangement of the body's various parts. It is an important reference point for adjusting vitality across the overall chakra structure.

Fifth Chakra Lop-sidedness:

A blocked throat chakra may exacerbate feelings of weakness, trepidation, and reflection. On the other end of the spectrum, an overactive throat chakra may cause tattling, constant talking, and being verbally strong or nasty. It may look like the conduit between the conversation in your head and what comes out of your lips is broken or non-existent.

An abnormality in the Throat Chakra might manifest as:
- Absence of power over one's speech; excessive or incorrect talking.
- Not being able to tune in to other people.
- Unreasonable fear of speaking, intangible voice.
- Not being able to retain secrets, to keep your statement.
- Lying

on the other hand,

A closed-throat chakra might manifest as excessive mystery or hesitancy.

In ordinary life, there is no relationship with a job or rationale.

The throat chakra represents the body's vocal component. It is a weight valve via which the imperativeness of the other chakra is transmitted.

If it is out of balance or obstructed, it might have an influence on the health of the other chakras.

When everything is in harmony, we can convey what we believe and feel. We may share our ideas, beliefs, and emotions. We may bring our own reality into the world when the throat chakra is consistent and open.

When the throat chakra is balanced, there is a fundamental movement of imperativeness inside the body and spirit. The imperativeness that rises from the sacral chakra via the sun-arranged plexus might continue its manner of engaging a free explanation of the features and necessities provided inside the imperativeness.

When the throat chakra is out of balance, bodily symptoms may include painful throats, tight jaws, a solid neck, and cerebral aches. When it is deeply out of balance, you may find yourself frequently lying, experiencing uneasiness and ambiguity about the intentions of others, or ending up stammering or silent. You will almost certainly feel constrained and misunderstood. You may be experiencing symptoms of various chakras being out of balance. This is caused by the throat chakra impeding the flow of life from various points.

1. The throat chakra will be unblocked and adjusted by blue gem vitality. The dismal blues have the intensity of reality. Lighter colors offer a higher level of flexibility, relaxation, and balance.

2. Yellow precious stones should be used to supplement the blue gem for a throat chakra adjustment. The exquisite yellow stones strengthen communication
and free articulation, taking vigor from the sun-powered plexus.

3. Sound therapy is often beneficial in unblocking the throat chakra. For maximum effectiveness, any precious stone-throat recuperation should be combined with soothing, melodious music.

CHAPTER 4: HEART CHAKRA

The heart chakra, or Anahata in Sanskrit, colors our life with empathy, love, and majesty.

The fourth vitality location is considered to unite natural and otherworldly aspirations since it is driven by the norms of change and joining.

Investigate what produces this chakra's pith and how to untangle its extraordinary vigor to improve your life.

Introducing the Heart Chakra, also known as Anahata.

<u>Chakra of the Heart Key Elements:</u>

Area: In the center of the chest (the vitality center is not located where our true heart is; rather, the heart chakra is located in the center of the chest territory). In the traditional seven-chakra system, it is the fourth chakra from the base of the spine.

<u>Green shading (higher vitality frequencies might become pink)</u>

Image: Two intersecting triangles frame a 6-pointed star with 12 petals.

Anahata is a unique Sanskrit name.

Air is a component.

Precious stones or gemstones, as well as scented healing, are additional components used in modern mending procedures to modify the heart chakra. In case you're curious, here's a summary of the most well-known ones for activating or adjusting the fourth chakra:

1. Mending stones for the heart chakra: pink quartz, transparent quartz, jade, and green calcite are all examples of gemstones.

2. Essential oils: rose, geranium, neroli, ylang-ylang, jasmine, bergamot

Make every cell in your body shiver and rejoice!

The bulk of us has energetic squares and awkward temperaments, as well as energy-subverting propensities that restrict us from reaching our maximum potential, causing us to feel empty, dejected, bored, and even ill.

Heart Chakra Essential Components:

Organs or significant capacities: Thymus organ, responsible for hormone production and important in the regulation of the immune system.

Psychological Meanings of the Heart Chakra:

The key implications or abilities associated with the heart chakra are as follows:

- Love for oneself as well as for others
- Relationships, connections
- Compassion and sympathy
- forgiveness, acceptance
- Change, change, change
- Capability to grieve and come to terms
- Insight into caring
- The focus of mindfulness, a collection of knowledge

When the heart chakra is open, you may feel deeply connected, a friendly exchange of vitality with everything around you, and an energy about excellence. In any event, when the heart chakra is blocked, you may have difficulties connecting to others, such as intense jealousy, co-dependency, or feeling shut off or pushed back.

Element of the Heart Chakra: Air Component: The fourth chakra is associated with the element of air.

Its life is linked to the breath and its developments, as is its ability to become huge and associate with all components.

Green is the color of the heart chakra.

Although many of us associate the color pink with the heart, this chakra is generally associated with the color green. The auric color of a functional fourth chakra may also be regarded as pink or smokey pink, therefore our popular depiction of love is a pink heart.

Chakra of the Heart

The Chest is the location.

The fourth chakra is most often associated with the center of the chest, between the bosoms. It is located on one side of the heart's actual organ. That's why it's referred to as the "heart chakra" so often.

Remember that the fourth vitality location is multidimensional and is talked to vivaciously with a front experiencing the focal point of the chest and a rear experiencing the spine between the shoulder bones.

The heart chakra is associated with the circulatory framework and the lungs due to its location. These organs are linked and rely on air and breathing to function properly.

The thymus is the organ associated with the heart chakra, and it is in charge of managing the invulnerable structure.

<u>The Chakra Symbol is:</u>

Traditionally, the picture representing the heart chakra is comprised of:

1. A twelve-petalled hover.
2. A descending pointing triangle is intertwined with an ascending pointing triangle to form a six-pointed star or hexagram.

The intersecting triangles represent the air component and its overall quality. They also represent the union of seemingly opposing principles or types of energy, such as masculine and female, soul and matter. The star that they build summons the peaceful union of forces and highlights the capability of the heart chakra as a focal point of mix and association. The twelve petals are commonly shown with the color red.

What exactly does Anahata mean?

The fourth chakra is also known as:
- The heart chakra
- Anahata
- Hritpankaja
- Dbadasjadala

The most well-known Sanskrit word for the heart chakra is "Anahata," which
means "unstruck."

What roles does the fourth Chakra play in everyday life?

The Heart Chakra is associated with mental and social characteristics such as:
- The ability to cherish.
- The combination is the connection between natural and supernatural desires.
- Rising above close-knit personality and inner-self constraints.
- Unlimited affection and connection with everyone.
- Insight from the heart.
- In every manner, energy is about splendor.
- Making important and necessary connections.

The lower and higher chakras are linked by the fourth chakra. As it were, the heart chakra serves as a focal point for the convergence of natural issues and higher goals. Far from judging things to be independent, the experience of the heart readily and agreeably coordinates them.

Associating and relating are associated with the Heart chakra. The emphasis here is on loving, giving, and accepting, as well as how open we are to seeing someone. Love is the energy that transforms sentiments and interactions. It is an essential component of every connection, whether with others or with oneself.

For what its worth, love experienced via the fourth chakra is about getting beyond the confines of self-image and individual diversions to open up more fully to empathy and acknowledgment of all that is. When we live from our hearts and our heart energy is open and tuned, we can see clearly and place ourselves in any situation, regardless of how difficult it is, with wit and empathy.

The heart chakra is also a center through which we encounter splendor in our daily lives. Seeing the universe through a reasonable fourth chakra is being in a state of receptiveness and recognition that brings us into touch with our reality and ourselves in meaningful and rewarding ways.

Signs your fourth Chakra may be out of balance:

The heart chakra may become unbalanced as a result of life experiences with a strong enthusiastic charge, physical problems, or significant changes in your health. It may manifest as an obstruction in the vitality stream or, contrary to popular belief, as a proclivity to become too busy or to have a surplus of energy.

Indications of Heart Chakra irregularity:
- Being too protective
- I'm feeling blocked.
- Envy; apprehension of proximity.
- Codependency is defined as relying on the approval and regard of others and

  seeking to please them at any cost.
- Constantly putting oneself in the shoes of a friend in need or a rescuer, or, despite what might be expected, falling victim to exploitation.
- Being a hermit requires unreasonable seclusion.
- Holding animosity and being unable to provide a justification.

<u>Physical manifestations include:</u>

Respiratory ailments such as lung contamination and bronchitis

Circulatory and cardiovascular problems

When the vitality in your fourth chakra is obstructed or stopped, you may experience what is often referred to as heart chakra pain.

<u>**Changes to the Heart Chakra:**</u>

To begin, consider the following simple practices:

Work with your breath to regulate your vitality; observe it and experiment with breathing exercises.

Develop your appreciation for greatness, whether in nature, persons, or human expressions.

Practice self-care and appreciate your body, from a good shower with rose essential oil to yoga poses that expand the heart area.

Develop self-empathy and acknowledgment, especially with regard to your emotions and body.

Participate in heart-healthy workouts.

Concentrate on obtaining if you're naturally inclined to be a provider; on providing

if you're more inclined to receive consistently.

Consider ancient family-related hurts and deal with them humanely; exercise

deep absolution inside your heart.

Offer your gratitude, whether it's calmly for the closeness of persons in your life

or just for useful items that make your life easier and happier.

Our emotions are physically present in our bodies. On a subtle level, our bodies communicate with the energies around us, and some eager driving impulses often correspond directly to a certain component of the body and chakra that is weakened or unbalanced. Each chakra represents an alien life practice or challenge that might help us get a better understanding of our own deep power. As a result, we must find out how to overcome obstacles, let go of passionate barriers, and travel the path to deep consciousness.

"Your task isn't to seek affection, but rather to seek and discover all the barriers within yourself that you have worked against." – Rumi

<u>**Fundamental Characteristics of the Heart Chakra:**</u>

The heart chakra is the human body's central powerhouse.

This is the point of convergence or scaffold that connects the three lower chakras associated with the outer world to the three higher chakras associated with instinct and otherworldliness. The heart is the intermediary between the body and the soul, and it directly determines their quality and well-being.

Love is the Heart Chakra:

The heart chakra, or Anahata, governs unconditional love and passionate power. This chakra is passionate at its core and urges us to develop our enthusiasm. The heart represents a sensitive shrewdness that demonstrates the techniques for devotion and empathy. We are just now realizing that the most powerful vitality on the planet is love.

The Anahata chakra resonates with our positive perception of the world.

The Heart Chakra is Pure:

This chakra is the focal point of a child's innocence and joy. When we were youngsters, we used to react to situations with a variety of emotions: assurance, compassion, love, anticipation, melancholy, and fear. However, as adults, producing feelings and being allowed to communicate them is extremely difficult. The Anahata awakens our capacity to love and let go; to accept our ardent desires while surrendering to an amazing arrangement.

What Does Our Heart Chakra Teach Us?

Surprisingly, the test of the heart chakra is largely the same as the challenges of the Solar Plexus (the third chakra), except that it communicates with us on a slightly more sophisticated level and is tuned in at a repetition that asks us to expand our compassion beyond our own self.

We detect a change in awareness in the Solar Plexus - a dual power of probing the self independently in the outer world and reflecting inward to more easily understand the notion of the self's presence inside the physical realm.

In contrast, the heart chakra thoroughly immerses itself in our intense emotions, as well as our interior world. It responds to interior thoughts, ideas, attitudes, motivation, and intense demands. If all of your chakras are aligned today, you will exude human energy, freely provide unfettered love, and form sound relationships.

The Heart Chakra's Power:

Unobtrusive (passionate) energy is thought to flow through our veins. As a result, if you allow pain and sharpness to overtake you, these bad energetic energies will cycle around your body and may destroy the whole body and spirit. In any event, if you can forgive and let go, allowing all that wants to be recorded in each breath and each cell, you will live with a glad heart.

We live in the organic effects of our natural choices as a whole - along these lines, we essentially determine whether to build a harsh heart or a kind heart.

We live in a civilization that has not yet healed the 'damaged child' inside, so painful memories and negative viewpoints despite everything plague us, creating a fractured mental self-portrait and keeping us living in the past. This passionate flotsam and jetsam must be separated from the heart and expelled through the root chakra. Actually, we have to get rid of that poop!

Indications of Heart Chakra Imbalance:

If this chakra is out of balance, one may suffer the negative impacts of desire, the inability to excuse others, and even become the abuser or mistreated seeing someone since adoration is power and some individuals use this capability to manipulate others.

Abusers need this control since their lower chakras are incapable of producing affection from their clan (Muladhara), companions (Sacral), and 'Self' (Solar Plexus).

Physical illness caused by a powerless Anahata can manifest as circularity issues and blood issues (as a result of being unable to circle love through oneself and other people), bosom disease, and heart disease (as a result of clutching deplorability or torment related to affection), an ailment in the lungs, stomach, and even suicide because the individual may not accept, they have the right to 'take in' adoring, all-inclusive life power (frequently allude

Essential trepidation sentiments that form in a misaligned heart chakra are being hesitant to follow your heart, despair, and obligation concerns. Throughout our lives, we must cultivate and strengthen our feelings of affection while also learning to forgive, be lenient, and have faith in our souls.

This is the Anahata quality: having the mental strength to love and empathize with ourselves and others, regardless of our circumstances.

Instructions for Healing Your Heart Chakra:

Consider love and forgiveness because they are inextricably linked: to admire is to excuse, and to forgive is to cherish. To attract a compassionate life force, practice Ujjayi Pranayama breathing. Express kindness, be generous, be thankful, and let go of the agonies stored in the heart.

1. Heart Chakra Yoga Poses: Cobra, Fish Pose, and Head to Knee Forward Bend.
2. Heart Chakra Precious Stones: Peridot, Rose Quartz, Lavender Kunzite
3. Heart Chakra Fragrant Healing: Rose, Melissa, Neroli

The heart chakra is the location of the heavenly fire in Taoism and Tantrism. Indeed, we perceive a blazingly open heart in works of art of Jesus, ready to spread out fast to each being right now. This is an update that, notwithstanding, we must forgive mistakes and ooze love since it is the finest vitality source capable of rising above all suffering and sadness.

Everything in our life is fueled by our heart's objectives. It is a part of the spirit's journey to confront what will shatter our hearts - not down the middle, but all the way open! The activity here is to consider what you will do with your misery. Will you blame it or will you rise above it and make an excuse? The heart is the path of incredible love and great insight. Is it fair to declare you're ready to stroll down this street?

This chapter investigates the Heart chakra's (the fourth chakra's) passionate and mental relationship with the physical world.

CHAPTER 5:SOLAR PLEXUS CHAKRA

The plexus chakra is located underneath the heart chakra, or more specifically the sacral chakra.

In any event, what does the sun-based plexus chakra say about you?

Here's all you need to know about this important chakra.

What is the Solar Plexus Chakra's Function?

Your solar plexus chakra is located over your navel and beneath your sternum. It serves as the center of energy for the inner self. It is simply the source of individual strength, conviction, and self-esteem.

When you:
- Gather the mental strength to do something that scares you, your sun-powered plexus chakra is activated.
- Take care of yourself.
- Use your willpower and discipline.
- You'll notice that your energy is strong in these situations, your posture is tall/commanding, and your voice is forceful.

The solar plexus chakra is the center of your own power.

Individual force, as it is now seen, does not imply power over others. It denotes self-authority - the ability to master your thoughts and emotions, overcome fear, and make the right decision in every situation.

Manipura, or sparkling gem,' is the Sanskrit term for the sun-based plexus.

Indeed, the sun-based plexus chakra enables you to meet the challenge at hand even when times are tough.

This chakra is referred to be a bright vivid yellow in shade. The shine of the sun-powered plexus chakra, like a beam of dawn, lights your path and warms your body with the brilliance of courage.

The sun-oriented plexus chakra allows you to pursue and not be distracted from your true path.

This chakra's energetic yellow handles creativity, character, insight, and self-image.

What are the symptoms of a blocked Solar Plexus Chakra?

Individuals with a powerless sun-based plexus chakra regard themselves as unfortunate victims. They walk skeptically with their heads down, with modest ambitions and objectives. They are shy and seldom hold positions of power, but they are quick to disparage others!

Tireless lack of bravery and self-esteem destroys their motivation to achieve anything meaningful in their life. As a result, they settle for a boring, perplexing presence.

It doesn't take much for the plexus chakra, which is built on sunshine, to become blocked or weakened. In fact, analysis and rejection are two of the strongest advocates for a blocked sun-oriented plexus chakra.

A few persons with insufficiency feelings will considerably overcompensate. This phony display of bragging and self-glorification might be interpreted as assurance or haughtiness. However, it is a forgery that easily disintegrates. This may lead to true misery and even more over-compensatory behavior.

Individuals with a strong sun-oriented plexus chakra don't brag about their accomplishments; instead, they let their results speak for themselves. They are firm yet kind.

A closed third chakra may manifest as physiological concerns as well.

Because of the location of this chakra in the center of the body, stomach disorders such as gas, queasiness, ulcers, diabetes, celiac disease, and liver disease are associated with a blocked sun-powered plexus chakra.

7 Methods for Opening the Solar Plexus Chakra:

Given the circumstances, what should you do if you suspect that your solar plexus chakra is blocked? **Here are seven suggestions for opening this chakra:**

1. Seek fresh interactions and astuteness to expand your knowledge and talents.
2. Move.
3. Do some yoga.
4. Consume yellow foods such as bananas, maize, and grains.
5. Consume natural teas.
6. Wear yellow and include yellow touches in your home decor.
7. Encourage yourself to break out of your usual routine by altering your daily agenda.

By removing yourself from your usual range of familiarity, you will begin to build common certainty. Being beyond our usual sphere of familiarity is disconcerting at first. However, it centers us to be present and stop overthinking.

The path to a healthy sunlight-based plexus chakra is striking a balance between being heard and overpowering people with phony demonstrations of assurance.

Allow your actions to speak for themselves. Discover the courage to make a move by focusing on your strengths and taking small proactive steps.

The Solar Plexus Chakra, which is placed between the belly and the solar plexus, is the core of our character, personality, and sense of self.

The third chakra is associated with self-discipline. While the Sacral chakra seeks joy and happiness, the third chakra is concerned with the perception of one's identity.

This chakra's characteristic is sensing your ability, and being certain, competent, and dependable.

The third chakra is the main point of your respect, resolve, self-control, and warmth as a character trait.

This chakra's vigor allows you to alter inactivity without reluctance and progress. It enables you to face challenges and go on in your life.

The main issue for the third chakra is to properly use your own ability.

What exactly does it mean? It entails consciously addressing the vitality of the solar plexus chakra. It indicates being proactive rather than reactive or inactive.

Creatures with high third-chakra energy react to life circumstances, have intense upheavals, and are constantly disturbed.

Creatures with a blocked or inadequate third chakra are distant and inactive, let life pass them by as they do nothing.

The solid third chakra represents the ability to go forward in life with assurance and power. It reflects the ability to make informed judgments to choose and act.

The third chakra's message is that you have the power to choose.

You may choose to fulfill your life purpose or to endure your karma or prior interactions.

What do you decide?

Do you choose to love, light, or rest?

Do you realize you have the capacity to choose?

Do you get a sense of opportunity when you make a decision?

Your attention is drawn to the third chakra.

When you pass judgment or criticize yourself, you deplete this chakra and weaken

your self-control.

The third chakra's structural squares are self-esteem, self-acknowledgment, and validation of your worth.

A woman with an open and balanced Manipura Chakra values herself and her work, believes in her ability to accomplish something admirably, cherishes and acknowledges herself, is eager to communicate intensely, and recognizes that she has the ability to act naturally and guide her own life.

Plexus Chakra Powered by the Sun Initially:

Manipura (jeweled city) is its Sanskrit name.

Fire is a component.

Shade: Yellow

Triangle with downward pointing

Lotus Petals with Ten Seeds Ram's sound:

Vowel Ah, sound.

The right to act

Adrenals and pancreas are endocrine organs.

Affiliation: Digestive framework, liver, and nerve bladder

Willpower: Mental Capacity

Personality: egocentric

Formative 18-42 month stage

Shame is the challenge.

Celestial aircraft is a kind of plane.

Sun and Mars are two planets.

Rudra and Laine are gods.

Imaginative Animal: Saffron, musk, and sandalwood make up Ram Incense.

Cinnamon and ginger are herbs.

Hod and Netzach from Sephora

Wands are the suit of the tarot.

Plexus Chakra Powered by the Sun Affirmations:

- I value and appreciate myself.
- I go up against myself.
- I am firm and fearless.
- I am worthy of admiration, consideration, and respect.
- I just choose the finest for myself.
- I speak up without hesitation.
- I am delighted with my achievements.
- I value myself.
- I choose solid connections.
- I am sincere.

- I am in charge of my own life.
- I am proud of my abilities.
- I am aware of my capability.
- In any case, I am free to choose.
- I search for opportunities for personal and professional growth.
- I'm happy with myself.

What exactly is the Solar Plexus Chakra?

This fiery chakra is associated with the color yellow. It governs your upper abdomen, between your navel and your breastbone.

What is the function of the Solar Plexus Chakra?

This chakra represents activity and change. It is associated with vigor, self-control, and the element of fire. It provides you with the VA boom you need to go forth in your daily life with confidence and clarity.

When the Solar Plexus Chakra is active, how do you feel?

You are focused and confident, ready for any exam. You are organized, cheerful, and capable of completing tasks.

A strong Solar Plexus Chakra urges you to stand up for yourself and create the life you want, rather than becoming entangled in the problems of others.

This area is also in charge of gut instinct. It may notify you soon if you've met the person you want to marry.

Or, more likely, warn you to avoid someone who is suspect.

When the Solar Plexus Chakra is atrophied:

When this chakra isn't properly fueled, you're like a lamp with a flattish battery: you don't sparkle brightly.

Everything appears to be too much. It is difficult to get yourself up in the morning and to make a mark on your calendar.

You could feel like a touch of the mat with your loved ones. Instead of stepping up to the plate, you may be grinding away at a routine task.

Could the Solar Plexus Chakra be overactive?

If you find it difficult to switch off, stress out excessively, or have difficulties sleeping, this chakra may be rotating too quickly. You may quiet it by shutting off your web-based social networking, going on a walk, attending a yoga class (a gentle one!), or spending a tranquil night at home doing nothing.

How can you balance and heal the Solar Plexus Chakra?

This chakra is associated with a lovely, dazzling, golden coloring, so whenever you see a dish of lemons or a shower of sunshine, it's a reminder of your solar plexus and how important it is.

Take several good, gentle yoga breaths deep into your stomach throughout the day.

How does this region make you feel?

You may feed this chakra by standing tall and feeling confident, and by consuming more yellow food (obviously, this is the nourishment we associate most with happiness). If you are facing major challenges, use positive self-talk to get through each step.

Could a Solar Plexus Chakra Bracelet Be of Assistance?

This chakra is represented as a triangle inside a lotus blossom. The triangle represents fire. Every time you see it shine on your wrist, it's a reminder that you can tap into the magnificent red-hot vigor of certainty and fearlessness.

The Solar Plexus Chakra is a good gift for...

Anybody who needs an extra tiny force pack of solidarity and assurance - maybe during testing, starting a new job or dealing with difficult people.

CHAPITRE 6: SACRAL PLEXUS CHAKRA

The Sacral Chakra, located in the pelvic area, is your fixation and enjoyment center. While the Root Chakra enjoys endurance, the second chakra seeks joy and happiness.

This chakra's endowment is interacting with our life via emotions and experiences.

The second chakra is the center of sensation, arousing quality, proximity, and affiliation.

The energy of this chakra allows you to give up, move, and experience the shift and change occurring inside your body. It allows you to appreciate this moment for what it is in its entirety.

The shaping of our general public is the fundamental test for the second chakra. We live in a society where feelings are not valued and where energy and strong answers are scorned. We have been told not to "give up control." Furthermore, we become disconnected from our bodies and emotions.

As if that weren't enough, we are also suffering the consequences of our collective societal conflicts over a variety of sexual problems in our society. On the one hand, sexuality is emphasized and praised, while on the other, it is ignored. This results in either obstructed or severe second chakra difficulties.

It's no wonder that we have so many concerns with our energy community, which is a fountain of emotions, pleasure, and exotic nature.

Do you appreciate your body? Do you like feeling your body? When was the last time you walked barefoot on the grass and felt the earth under your feet?

The sacral chakra is also your source of creative energy.

Enthusiasm is the driving force of inventive liveliness. Everything you create, whether it's a sonnet, a drawing, or a website, stems from the vitality of the second chakra. It is also where your ripeness begins. Imagining a child is an imaginative process.

A person with an open Svadhisthana Chakra is active, present in her body, stimulating, inventive, and linked to her predilection.

<u>Sacral Chakra at first:</u>

Svadhisthana is the Sanskrit name for this place.

Water is an essential component.

Orange shading

Circle with sickle shape

Lotus Petals with Six

Seeds VOICE: VANG

Oo is a vowel sound.

Rights to Believe: The right to believe and the need to believe

Ovaries and gonads are endocrine organs.

The womb, privates, kidney, and bladder are all physically related.

Movement and association are examples of mental abilities.

Personality: Emotional

Formative Stage: 6 months to 2 years

Guilt is a difficult challenge.

An astral plane is a kind of aircraft.

Mercury, Jupiter, and the Moon are the planets.

Indra, Rakini, and Vishnu are the gods.

Gardenia and damiana incense

Fennel and coriander are herbs.

Yesod at Sephora

Tarot Cups suit

Chakra Sacral Affirmations:

- I value and take care of my physique.
- I have clear boundaries.
- I am open to experiencing the present moment via my abilities.
- I have a lot of energy.
- With each breath I take, I am filled with joy and wealth.
- I nurture my body with solid food and clean water.
- I understand how to meet my needs.
- I value and respect my body.
- I am open to interaction and connection.
- I allow myself to experience a delight.
- My sexuality has been sanctified.
- My spirit communicates via my feelings.
- I am very conscious of my physical body.
- I've made my decision.

The chakras correspond to our bodies' force points and are vertically adjusted from the base of the spine to the crown of the skull. In Sanskrit, the second chakra in **our body is known as Svadhisthana**, which **means "sweetness."** It is also known as the sacral chakra and is located in two fingers under the coccyx or tailbone.

The chakra framework was initially recognized as the formation of specific Hindu, Buddhist, and Taoist teachings in the Orient. The chakras are what these civilizations refer to as the human soul's living systems.

What is Svadhisthana, often known as the Sacral Chakra?

Svadhisthana is about growth, flow, caring, joy, sexuality, relationships, and reproduction. It alludes to our masculine and female polarities. It is related to building blissful, satisfying, and loving interactions.

The sacral chakra's energy stores desires, emotions, and sensations. The society in which we live does not encourage us to behave normally, to experience, and convey our emotions. As a result, we must learn to control our emotions and desires from a young age. We are told not to weep, not to talk freely, and not to be ashamed of our sexuality. This stifled vitality remains trapped in the second chakra, resulting in uneven characters.

Furthermore, the sacral chakra stores our alleged "shadow" or clouded side. Every one of those things that we don't care about. They, however, cannot be avoided and may continue to appear in our lives in some way. "The Shadow" manifests itself most often in the broken relationships we have or in a broad variety of scenarios that reoccur again.

When we begin working with our sacral chakra, we must manage our suppressed feelings and feelings of blame and disgrace. We will also need to address and accept our flaws, understanding that they contribute to who we actually are and assist us to be whole. Only when we reach this realization will we be able to find relief?

How Can You Tell If Your Sacral Chakra Is Blocked?

When your sacral chakra is balanced, you become intelligent, industrious, and unconstrained. You are full of creative energy and are uninhibited, liberated, and happy.

When this chakra is out of balance, you may notice the following symptoms:
- Ingenuity is lacking.
- Connectors that are dull or broken. You may encounter unpleasant experiences repeatedly.
- Inspiration is lacking.
- Absence of sexual desire or horrible sex.
- Passionate disarray
- You are feeling unimportant.
- You believe that no one loves you.
- You believe you are not accepted by those around you or by the wider public.
- You reason that you don't know how or that you can't cope with yourself.

If your sacral chakra is excessively active, you are an obsessive worker, preferring seeing someone, ravenous, fixated on delight, and reliant on a wide variety of workouts that you employ as a replacement for adoration.

<u>Methods for Sacral Chakra Healing:</u>

If you often hang or have your shoulders twisted, it is most likely due to an unhealed sacral chakra. Carrying your shoulders forward is an attempt to conceal your chest or sexuality.

It may also be a move to protect your heart chakra. If you straighten your shoulders and open your chest, your heart chakra will open, and it will be too difficult to tolerate all of the unhealed anguish. Regardless, the sacral chakra is joined at the hip with the heart chakra because both are associated with suppressed feelings and unhealed injuries.

To boost your sacral chakra, make the following changes in your life:
- **Take care of yourself:**

Rest sufficiently, consume nutritious foods, and clean up if it helps you relax.

Make an attempt to visit a spa on occasion.

●Be patient with yourself:

Try not to overthink every action you make.

●Be close to the water:

Keep a watchful eye on the way

Whether beside the beach, stream, or lake, anything related to water may be beneficial.

●Drink plenty of fluids:

Drink plenty of water, fresh juices, and soups.

●Concentrate on your extracurricular activities:

These can be any exercises that help you to release your imagination.

Engage in tantric intercourse:

As a result, have intercourse with a lot of care and attention. Consider sex to be sacred.

Restore or discontinue harmful connections:

Never again maintain relationships with people who do not progress or support your growth. If there are unresolved issues or implied dissatisfactions, be open and peaceful in resolving them.

Balance your male and female energies:

There are a few processes you may try to balance your male and female energies. Hip opening or hip revolution yoga techniques are incredible.

Unrestricted motion:

You might also try an unrestricted move in which you allow your body to follow the rhythm of the music to aid you in releasing the blocked energy.

Remember that change starts on the inside:

If you want to increase your mind-blowing nature, you must first understand what creates uncomfortable nature in your sacral chakra. At that moment, you must silently remove any deterrent.

What is the Sacral Chakra in charge of?

The sacral chakra is said to regulate passionate parity, explicit excitement, sexuality, and relationships. This includes both dreams and ingenuity. The sacral chakra restricts all sensations, whether physical, deep, or passionate.

Delight and the ability to experience it are already formed; taking responsibility for this key control position might increase your psychological flexibility.

In general, the sacral chakra is an important part of everyday life.

Sacral Chakra Imbalance Symptoms:
Because the sacral chakra is responsible for enthusiastic and sexy equalization, sacral awkwardness affects many aspects of your life. Some signs of this are problems with relationships and freedom. You can end yourself dreaming in inappropriate ways if you don't make a move. A closed chakra may elicit feelings of lack and alienation from emotion.

The following are some signs of Sacral Chakra Awkwardness:
- Misery
- Self-Doubt
- Dysfunction of the sex
- Addiction

While some of these symptoms may be caused by everyday circumstances, a sacral chakra imbalance may be adding to your stress. A blocked chakra manifests itself in a variety of structures that are not easily discernible.

Sometimes the side effects of a sacral irregularity appear gradually. Do you ever feel that it's becoming more difficult to fully participate in activities that make you happy? Perhaps you have a sacral irregularity that prevents you from acting on your feelings and pursuing your interests. Rather, you may end up with the misguided impression that everything is fine and fail to stand up to your feelings, resulting in much more intense trouble.

Instructions for Rebalancing Your Sacral Chakra:
Since we've discussed the effects of a blocked sacral chakra, let's talk about how to rebalance it and get the most out of your inward vitality.

When the sacral chakras are open, people are more aware of their emotions and what they need to accomplish—this results in a more fulfilling existence because of an improved sense of direction.

Before we go into more specific ways to rebalance your sacral chakra, remember that one of the greatest ways to rebalance your sacral chakra is just doing activities you discover you like. You sometimes neglect the things that satisfy you in the midst of the chaos of everyday life. You may begin to heal your unbalanced chakra by reconnecting to your fundamental roots and performing activities that you know would delight you.

Additional exercises for rebalancing your Sacral Chakra include:
- Contemplating
- Back massages
- Reciting
- Care

Pelvic pushes and cobra yoga are two mindful movements that are specifically for your sacral chakra. Sun greetings provide a double benefit. The introspection alone helps in rebalancing, and starting your day with silence prepares you for a day of substantial, gratifying partnerships.

Back massages and needle treatment have also helped with pressure and rebalancing, resulting in a more balanced sacral chakra. Maintaining a clear mind and reasoning contributes to the rebalancing method since you will begin balancing the effects of an unbalanced chakra right away.

In conclusion, the sacral chakra impacts many aspects of life, therefore engaging in the suggested rebalancing actions may result in a more meaningful and joyful existence. Staying in touch with your emotions and opening yourself up to new experiences will allow you to rebalance your sacral chakra and improve your life.

CHAPTER 7: ROOT CHAKRA

The first chakra, often known as the root chakra, is located at the base of the spine. The perineum, along the first three vertebrae, and the pelvic plexus are the corresponding bodily regions. This chakra is often described as a cone of energy that begins at the base of the spine and descends before being delicately twisted up.

Root Chakra Characteristics:

The first Chakra is associated with accompanying abilities or social traits like:

- Security and well-being.
- Endurance.
- Nutrition, rest, cover, self-preservation, and other basic necessities
- The rawness, physicality, and aspects of oneself.
- Establishing.
- Establishment of our way of life.

Make every cell in your body shiver and rejoice!

The majority of us have robust squares and unbalanced features, as well as energy-undermining proclivities that impede us from reaching our full essentialness, causing us to feel empty, spent, dull... even ill.

The root chakra provides the foundation around which we build our lives. It aids us in growing and gaining confidence in researching all aspects of life. It is associated with our sense of well-being and security, regardless of whether it is physical or in relation to our basic necessities, or symbolic in relation to dwelling and monetary well-being. To recap, the first chakra questions are about the potential for endurance and well-being. The root chakra is where we connect to the soil and wrestle our energy into the visible world.

What occurs when the First Chakra is out of balance?

At the passionate level, the deficiencies in the first Chakra were recognized as:

- Extreme pessimism and criticism
- Dietary concerns
- Dream
- Covetousness and voracity
- Overwhelming feelings of insecurity, always operating in endurance mode.

For someone who has lopsidedness in the first chakra, it may be difficult to feel secure on the planet, since everything seems to be a possible peril. The need for security commands may transform into concerns about the activity situation, bodily well-being, cover, and well-being. A blocked root chakra might lead to practices that are mostly governed by fear.

Similarly, when the root chakra is hyperactive, fear may morph into greed and distrustfulness, both of which are extreme manifestations of a first chakra imbalance. It is associated with issues with control over nutrition intake and diet.

Awaken your Sacral and Root Chakras!

The Root and Sacral Chakras are inextricably linked to our sexuality.

Learning how to develop and master our sexuality may so stimulate, initiate, and strengthen these Chakras.

Chakra of the Root:

Activating the Root Chakra:

There are several methods for opening your root chakra. For example, you may link more in establishing earth-related workouts (such as nature association, farming, cooking sound, and climbing).

The main idea is to focus on establishing your "underlying foundations" in a safe and pleasing environment (i.e., surround yourself with earthy colors, items that remind you of nature, and dependability; alternatively, if you want to feel less trapped, do the contrary).

Yoga for the root chakra may be a more physical way to connect the body and mind

and re-establishing a more regulated energy flow.

What is the meaning of the word Muladhara or Root Chakra?

The first chakra is known as:
- The Root chakra.
- Muladhara
- Adhara

The Sanskrit term "Muladhara" may mean "base", "establishment", or "root support".

Component: Earth

Chakra Colors: The chakra of red

A deep vermilion red is a typical coloring used to communicate with the root chakra. This is the shading used to fill the petals in its picture.

It is also associated with the color yellow or gold (this is the color of its composition rather than its petals). Red is a chakra color that represents quality, and imperativeness, and invigorates our innate proclivities.

Image of the Root Chakra:

The root chakra is represented by a four-petaled lotus bloom, which is commonly modified as a hover with four petals and a downward-pointing triangle.

The downward-pointed triangle represents the soul connecting with the problem, establishing on the ground, and our natural existence in our bodies. It is regarded as the center point of our essential life force and is where kundalini stays wound and dormant until it wakes to transmit its energy via the different chakras.

The Matter Chakras:

The first three chakras, originating at the base of the spine, are problem chakras. They are becoming more physical.

We shall begin with the first Matter-Root Chakra, Mūlādhāra.

In Sanskrit, the Root Chakra is known as Mūlādhāra. The Root Chakra is the first of our energy centers, and it serves as the foundation and starting point for our progress. The key life and vitality of the Root Chakra begin from conception. Embryogenesis continues with life force vitality separating the phones. The spinal segment begins to form from the bottom (root chakra) to the top (crown chakra), and then organs form.

The Root Chakra is associated with the major task we perform following birth, which is to determine "Do I have a place here?"... on this Earth and right now. It's not a deliberate investigation based on (thinking) insight. It comes naturally.

Root chakra— Mūlādhāra is the most instinctive of all chakras; it is your place of endurance. The fundamental vitality of endurance is the fight, flee, or freeze reflex, which begins with Root chakra vitality. This is your animal nature of perseverance.

This is the chakra that governs our animal nature and reflects the sublime endurance sensation of scent, and later, taste. This is the child's primitive sensing of the world, sometimes referred to as "establishing," when the infant moves her/his head, 'establishing' around and detecting her/his approach to nutrition via its mouth and sense of smell. If this basic endurance need is met, the baby will legitimately move to the article without looking.

Furthermore, the baby discovered his/her first crude confirmation that he/she belongs right now, which will strengthen endurance.

When considering analyst Erik Erickson's stages of development, the major stage—trust versus question—is strongly associated with Root chakra growth. As an infant, if your parental figures consistently provided you with what you expected to endure (food, water, love, companionship, and joyful silence), you felt secure in the world. You believed that the world could be relied on to provide your basic requirements. However, if your condition was confused and parental figures were depressed to you, and additionally if your guardians delayed, postponed, or were conflicting in giving you what you required, you will require trust and security and may end up with Root chakra irregularity or blockages. Whether or whether you feel secure now is significantly influenced by how safe you felt when you were a child.

The root chakra— Mūlādhāra—is the chakra of dependability, security, and our basic requirements. The root chakra is important in whatever grounding you have in your life. This incorporates your basic requirements, for example, nutrition, water, cover, and wellness, as well as your passionate wants of connection and bravery. When these needs are satisfied, you will feel grounded and protected.

It is the most important Chakra since it is the Fundamental (or Mool) Chakra.

The Root Chakra is associated with the physical body, which includes the adrenal organs, colon, kidneys, skeleton/bones, muscles, and blood vascular blood that circulates via the left chamber of the heart, carrying oxygen and vitamins to human bodily tissue.

The Root Chakra is responsible for connecting our fiery structure to the physical universe. It is the foundation of our vigor and life force. It motivates us to eat, sleep, and reproduce. In terms of our mental and deep nature, it motivates us to strengthen our trustworthiness, confidence, and sense of belonging.

The energies of the Root Chakra assist us in feeling grounded and connected to this Earth, providing a space for our life to 'flourish' and for the evolution of energies to take us forward on our life journey. When these energies become trapped, stale, unbalanced, or hampered, our vitality and pizzazz are also undermined. This might happen when our sense of belonging on the earth is disrupted in some way or is seen as horrifying, leaving us with a strong sense of insecurity.

Unevenness in life and vitality in the Root Chakra might leave us feeling eager or facing a lack of vitality, which may manifest as anxiousness, tension, panic, discouragement, disappointment, hate, outrage/rage, or a lack of passion for the world or in our perseverance. We may also confront indicators such as being undermined, always feeling as if we don't belong in or have a place, and experiencing weakness and poor confidence. Mental symptoms include a weak center, disruption, pessimism, negative life contemplation, and restricted thinking.

However, when the Root Chakra is adjusted and vitality can flow freely, it encourages us to increase the feeling of belonging, and safety in our activities and decisions and can hold an expanded sense of self-esteem. Mental: Improved concentration, diligence, dependable judgment, ability to define goals, and ability to organize. Passionate means full of excitement, affection, energy, and certainty.

The journey to repair physical/mental injuries housed in the Root chakra is aided by more depth treatment with psychotherapy (for example, injury psychotherapy), Reiki-Tummo, precise yoga asanas, judo, and growth introspection that evacuates stagnant gathered excited energy.

The vitality of the Root chakra enables us to deal with mental bravery, ingenuity, and the desire to survive amid difficult situations. The root chakra connects us to the deep energy of our forefathers' and foremothers' problems and successes. Because the Root Chakra conveys our ancestors' memories, everyone encounters difficulties or awkward nature inside the Root Chakra.

War, famine, apocalyptic disasters, and any other occurrences that impair our basic endurance are stored inside the Root chakra energies. These memories are imprinted in the inconspicuous body (i.e., life energy). They are passed down from generation to generation, creating oblivious generational examples. It is our responsibility to accept responsibility for our own lives and to expose what is oblivious or idle.

Karmas from past lives and present life, Karma, like seeds, are also stored in the Root Chakra's vitality field.

When the circumstances are satisfied, the seeds/energies that were sown will show/present/emerge in a variety of structures: mental, emotional, mental, physical, and otherworldly.

Each thought, purpose, or deed that we execute or have performed plants a seed in the Root Chakra, which will ultimately climb into the light. We have sown several seeds throughout our lives.

Mūlādhāra, the first of the seven essential habitats, is also the thickest of the seven chakras. The primary color of this chakra is red, which is also the darkest of all chakra colors.

Red is the slowest of the visible spectrum's wavelengths, but it is the most energizing shade. It draws the retina forward, directing all of our vigor and attention outward.

That is why we use the color red for stoplights and stop signs. Consideration is ordered by the root chakra shade. It represents a danger to us. We take immediate action. The color red represents the presence of power. It is the color of blood and the first color we come into touch with when we are created. Read the method's energy and our relationship with the Earth, and it offers the assurance of endurance.

The Mūlādhāra Chakra's Bīja Mantra (Seed Mantra) is LM, the sound of intense arousal. It now activates its energy by releasing stresses and expelling impediments. Thus begins the process of awakening the dormant powers within us and bringing them to consciousness. Beautiful and healing meetings, as well as joyful moments, emerge from the past, energizing and motivating us to continue on our path. However, in addition to charming encounters, we can also have agonizing feelings in the Mūlādhāra Chakra. Covered damages, natural passionate hurts, and frustrations that were deeply scratched into our consciousness emerge to the surface so they may finally be recuperated and resolved.

Dissatisfaction is not a bad emotion, but it does indicate a shift in our progress and knowledge. Each learning step in our lives is connected by the correction of a false belief, by "dissatisfaction." Excruciating disappointments regularly fill the MūlādhāraChakra to overflowing. However, when we approach these disasters with intelligence, they transform into significant encounters and opportunities for advancement.

We shall be confronted with problems for the rest of our lives. The uneducated regard them as an annoyance and a setback, but the observant sees them as crucial and beneficial experiences. We grow in our deep development when we learn from them and begin to chip away at ourselves. If we don't accomplish this, we will be trapped in our agony, repeating the agonizing exercises.

Mūlādhāra is the first chakra.

The seven chakras are very important and associated with one another. Normally, adjusting one chakra causes a change in another. However, it is critical to first adjust the Root Chakra before moving on to other people, or we will lack the strength and rootedness required for genuine change and self-awareness.

We can't grow and evolve until we have a feeling of safety and security. Mūlādhāra is in charge of endurance.

Muladhara means "root support" in Sanskrit.

•Mūla = Origin, Root, Essence

•Ādhāra = Foundation, Basis

Coccyx and the first three vertebrae at the base of the spine.

Adrenal cortex/adrenal organs (battle flight) Endocrine Organ

Bladder, colon/digestive organ, bone, foot, leg, teeth, blood artery lifeblood to the left office of the heart

Formative Stage: From birth to a year.

Adjusted/ Streaming vitality: When this chakra is open/vitality is streaming, we feel safe and courageous in the world.

Imbalanced: The Root Chakra is hampered by fear and many sorts of harm. Drowsiness, nutritional problem.

Mental symptoms of blockage include:

Uneasiness, dread, panic attacks, stress, overthinking, depression, terrible nightmares, being really disconnected, being divided from the body, and outrage/rage.

Physical symptoms of a blockage include:

Dormancy and actual depletion, problems with the colon, bladder, end or with the lower back, problems with the left arm, leg, or foot, inflammation, and cramping. Prostate problems may occur in males. Dietary issues may also be a symptom of a root chakra imbalance.

The Root Chakra governs our bodily energy, providing us with a sense of well-being and security with others, ourselves, and confidants in daily life. Without modifying it, no matter how hard we try, higher chakras cannot be recovered/unblocked/streamed till the Root chakra— Mūlādhāra is flowing.

Component: (Earth is our mother, and our bodies are made out of her components. She supports and feeds us)

Syllabus of Mantra Seeds: LAM

Red shading

Our various mental states and emotions are defined by certain Chakra shading frequencies. Red is a frequent occurrence.

Bodhisattva: Red Tara represents compassion.

Amitabha: The totals of acumen, untainted recognition, and considerable awareness of the shunyata of all things.

Tactile: The sense of smell (olfaction).

Changing the Root Chakra- Mūlādhāra

Garnet, crimson jasper, dark tourmaline, and bloodstone are the stones/gems.

While resting, place the gemstone on the chakra region to help open and adjust it. Wear it, on the other hand.

Physical activity (Yang and Yin)

Eating red natural goods (beets, tomatoes, strawberries, and fruits) for nutrition.

Interfacing with the ground, walking barefoot on the grass, and farming are just a few examples of root chakra activities.

Mending vibrations/Sound showers with specific repetition to the Root chakra. Our various mental states and emotions are characterized by certain Chakra sound frequencies. When exposed to a complete Chakra sound recurrence for a long enough period of time, the Chakras will be brought into balance, and when your Chakras are in harmony, so are your mind and emotions. My YouTube channel offers playlists for Sound baths and a specific Chakras vitality recuperation that I recommend based on four years of clinical mending study.

Asana (yoga pose):
   * Pavanamuktasana—knee to chest present
   * Janu Sirsansana—head to knee pose
   * Padmasana—lotus flexion
   * Malasana—hunching down posture
   * Tadasana — mountain present
   * Shavasana — carcass present
   * Virabhadrasana I — Warrior I (*this is a yang present, but it fortifies mental fortitude, try to stand shoeless on

Meditation Development for Blockage Removal:
Reflection not only links you to a greater deep dimension, but it also helps to ground you. You may not have the choice of believing that the world would give you what you have to suffer. However, association with your higher self and trust in a force greater than yourself will provide you with the security you seek.

Psychotherapy techniques include:

Interpersonal, Psychodynamic, Object Relations, and Contemplative for the root cause(s) and combination for mending, as well as explicit social responses for side effect indicators.

1. Reiki-Tummo Vitality Restoring Oils: *Sandalwood, Rosewood, Rosemary, Black Pepper, Cedar, Clove, Ginger, Frankincense, Myrrh
2. Mūlādhāra,

the First Root Chakra Affirmations:
   • I'm feeling concentrated.
   • I am now at home.
   • I am connected to my body.
   • My body is my residence.

•I'm feeling secure.

•My virtues are truth and equality, which I represent.

•I have everything I need.

•I am kind and forgiving to myself.

•I have endless possibilities.

•I am grateful for trials because they help me to become more grounded.

•I am daring.

•I open myself to myself.

•I'm in love with myself.

•I confide in the obvious source, which is a widely ideal mother who meets my

basic requirements.

•I fuel myself properly, drink clean water, breathe clean air, exercise, relax, and

spend time in nature.

Muladhara, or the Root Chakra, is the first chakra. Each chakra corresponds to a different part of the body and different aspects of ourselves. The Root Chakra, being the first chakra, plays an important role in our lives and how we relate to our general environment.

Our emotions are physically present in our bodies. On a subtle level, our bodies communicate with the energies around us, and particular intense motivations, for the most part, genuinely tie to a specific piece of the body and chakra that is debilitated or unbalanced.

Each chakra represents an alien life practice or challenge that might help us get a better understanding of our own deep power. As a result, we must find out how to overcome obstacles, let go of passionate impediments, and travel the path to deep consciousness.

"There is profound insight inside our very tissue if we can just wake up and feel it." Behnke, Elizabeth A.

The first chakra is called by many names, including root, base, and Muladhara.

In Sanskrit, "Muladhara" means "establishment."

The Root Chakra keeps us anchored and connected to ancestral beliefs that aid in the early formation of character and a sense of belonging. The Muladhara's vitality is an ancestral energy. It's all about relationship quirks and basic wants like feeling secure, which are boosted and met.

The following are the Root Chakra's Fundamental Qualities:

The Muladhara chakra corresponds to "Who am I corresponding to other people?" We all need that essential encouraging group of folks - it's imprinted in our early-stage cerebrums in order to survive.

We are naturally exposed to - and continue to seek - this gathering having a place throughout our lives.

When modified under acceptable circumstances, the Root Chakra energizes security in bigger groupings. It caters to lives' basic demands, such as feeling comfortable, supported within your family, and recognizing you can develop a sense of self.

The Root Chakra is intuitive:

The primary focus of the first chakra is sustenance, sex, refuge, and endurance. It even encompasses reliability and regard for the "pack." The desire to feed on or throng material goods and currency is a bad expression of our enduring nature.

If our basic requirements are not met (for example, we believe we are not receiving enough sustenance, income, product, or sex to satisfy that yearning), our Muladhara is rendered ineffective. This suggests that we are fully integrated with the planet.

The Root Chakra is the emotional and mental health foundation.

If the energetic and mental power within your youth relationship complication was (and still is) acceptable, you will have a decent root chakra with robust endurance senses that can resist the problems of grown-up existence.

Different psychological instabilities are formed as a result of early unfavorable family contacts, and they might cause additional disruptions in the upper chakras when the first chakra is out of balance.

The Root Chakra is our auric field's lively reusing container.

Intense Muladhara-related topics might lead to bodily illnesses since we feel vulnerable and rejected by our tribe. This may include a resistant-related concern.

What Can the Root Chakra Teach Us?

The Muladhara Chakra practice is to have the will to break free from the passionate enslavement that holds you back.

If you can't find individual flexibility, you'll end up carrying a lot of psychological weight into your jobs and future relationships.

As a result, your perception of the current world is distorted.

Living becomes perilous and perilous since the passionate institutions were not properly formed within you from the start.

The Root Chakra's Power:

The Root Chakra, being the vibrant reusing receptacle of our auric field, converts negative passionate emotions into energy and light.

The chakra then returns this to the land as lively fertilizer. We can't get rid of waste energy if our roots are disconnected from the soil and our underlying motives are out of harmony.

Allow everything to wash away in the dirt. Before these vibrant concerns may channel up the upper chakras, we must let go of some ideas that might be detrimental.

The Root Chakra is our initial understanding of love and perseverance, and it is critical to our journey that we recover any obstructions from our foundations.

The Muladhara is an ideal early stage, with a natural ladylike energy. It is the intensity of touch while making adoration. It is the caring warmth and love that we provide to our children. The Root Chakra is the foundation of life, and it encourages us to reproduce and express physical and powerful love to people we care about.

We sometimes forget the importance of the Root Chakra (or, when all is said and done, the chakras for certain people). Yogis will generally focus more on the upper chakras to achieve enlightenment or a sense of harmony. Regardless, how can we achieve harmony if our institutions are weak? How can a tree stand tall and happy if it has no roots to aid its development?

<u>**Indications of Root Chakra Imbalance:**</u>

When the Root Chakra is out of balance, you may notice the following symptoms:

1. Skeletal abnormalities resulting from the lack of assistance from the collective family body
2. Intestinal scatters when the waste cannot be reused.
3. Conceptual difficulties stem from a sense of being unworthy of a loving family.

Root Chakra irregularity might cause meditations or acts based on a sense of need (for example, stockpiling, overeating, and so on). Awkwardness produces severe subjects stemming from a lack of ability to feel grounded, as well as sexual troubles stemming from vivacious obstruction or prior injuries.

The following are step-by-step instructions for healing your Root Chakra:

This life drug should be applied to your Root Chakra. Move to the rhythm of a drum, take a walk-in nature, sow seeds, feel the dirt between your toes, and forgive the past. Do activities that will make you feel anchored. Praise the people in your life that you care about and who make you feel protected.

Assist your first chakra using the postures, precious stones, and essential oils listed below.

1. Warrior One, Triangle Pose, and Eagle Pose are yoga poses for the Root Chakra.

Carnelian and Bloodstone are two precious stones that may help balance the Root Chakra.

3. Fragrant healing for the Root Chakra: Cedarwood, Patchouli, Myrrh

The Root Chakra represents our potential to grow. We emerge from the muck like a lotus flower by allowing our distinctive sentiments to flourish.

When you find balance in your Root Chakra, you find equilibrium in all aspects of your life. It all starts with the first chakra!

The Root Chakra (Muladhara) is located at the base of the spine and is associated with our sense of endurance, security, and autonomy. When the root chakra is balanced, we feel stable, safe, and full of vigor, wellness, and soundness. When the root chakra is shaky, we may feel easily agitated, ungrounded, and depleted of vigor.

The most effective way to become grounded is:

There aren't many ways to cleanse, heal, and energize the root chakra. Using precious stone therapy is an excellent way to feel grounded. Bloodstone, garnet, ruby, jasper, and smokey quartz are powerful establishing stones that can help you become more peaceful and concentrated. Try carrying about a few of these stones to get more linked with the ground.

Sustain your Root Chakra:

Another way to chakra maintenance is sustenance. To modify and revitalize your root chakra, include red apples, raspberries, grapes, strawberries, pomegranates, beets, and watermelon into your diet.

Yoga for the Ground:

Tadasana (Mountain Pose), Uttanasana (Forward Bend), and Virabhadrasana (Warrior 1) are the finest yoga poses for connecting you to your earth chakra. Each of these positions connects us to the ground and helps us put our consciousness back into the physical body.

Connect with the Earth:

Because the root chakra's component is earth, just going out into nature and sitting in a position where you can feel the ground under you will have a healing effect. Allow the vibrations of the earth beneath you to travel up your lively spine and out into all of your appendages.

Imagine a beautiful crimson bundle of life softly sparkling at the base of your spine as you meditate on your root chakra.

Allow that vitality to ascend the body and repeat the mantra "I am." I have a home. I am silent and concentrated. "May the vitality of the earth restore my imperativeness."

We will look at ways to heal, stimulate, and cleanse each of the seven chakras. Continue reading.

I'm sending you lots of love and light.

CHAPITRE 8: OPENING YOUR CHAKRA

Opening the chakras is feasible in a variety of methods for various problems.

Here's some easy advice on how to awaken your chakras in three stages:
  Stage 1: Understand your chakras
  Stage 2: Determine which chakras are the most important to open initially.
  Stage 3: Activate the vitality needed to open the chakra.

There are several methods for opening chakras; some are advocated by conventional schools of thought associated with Eastern otherworldliness; others are increasingly presenting and are routinely prepared from these increasingly ancient traditions.

They were created by people who are interested in brain research, healing, and all-encompassing medicine to aid us in our routine day-to-day lives. We shall unearth, for the most part, modern notions and ways that you may easily use on your own.

Activating the Chakras Step 1: Understand Your Chakras

Knowing your chakras is the first step in opening them. These concentrations of energy have distinct properties and qualities that are useful in perceiving or locating higher comparability. Practices to open the root chakra, for example, will differ from those used to open the heart or third eye chakras. We were familiar with the chakras in the preceding seven chapters.

Make every cell in your body move and rejoice!

The significance most of us have energetic squares and unbalanced features, as well as vitality disruptive tendencies that limit us from acquiring our maximum imperativeness, causing us to feel exhausted, scattered, dull... even unwell.

Understand your chakras as an activity. Go online and learn about the seven chakras and their unique properties.

Activating the Chakras Step 2: Determine which Chakra needs the greatest assistance.

The next step is determining which chakra has to be addressed initially. The chakras are inextricably linked. If one chakra is out of balance, whether it is overactive and excessively open or insufficient and shut, or vitality does not flow well through it, the neighboring chakras and the entire framework may be influenced. As a result, it might be difficult to determine which chakra requires the most attention at times.

Here are a few pointers:

Take the chakra test; it will help you identify possible areas to focus on.

Examine whether you have a confined physical torment; it may be associated with

the movement of the chakra associated with that region.

Examine what's going on and what's typically risky or causes the greatest anxiety

(for example, a relationship, money, a sense of well-being, a lack of inspiration,

an eager thrill ride, and so on.)

Examine a person who is aware of one's vitality.

Be aware of a few of the chakras that need to be opened initially. Take a chakra test to see which chakras need the most attention.

Chakra Activation:

Activating the Chakras Step 3: Use Vitality to Open Your Chakra.

The third stage is to specify the vitality in the chakra that has to be opened.

It's useful to think about it in terms of "opening" your chakra, but also of re-establishing flow, developing acquaintance with its condition and variety, and modifying input and outflow of energy. When opening your chakras, the fundamental guideline at work is equalization or adjusting.

You may practice the following to activate the vitality in the chakras you want to open:

•Physical activity focused on the chakra region of the body

•Breathing exercises

•Meditation on a certain chakra

•Reflection and self-request to address the mental and emotional blocks

•Hands-on self-healing methods (for example, rub, "chakra association" technique)

•Restore your chakras by attending a meeting.

When you start initiating vitality in a chakra that has an irregularity, "stuff" may come up. The "stuff" that was contributing to chakra closure may now travel to your awareness, giving you the chance to handle it more thoughtfully. Take care of yourself by giving yourself ample rest, moments of introspection, and thinking, as well as physical exercise to keep things flowing.

For many years, the traditional teachings of Hinduism and Buddhism have comprehended the concept that etheric life focused on the body known as chakras. These centers put life force and underlying vitality into bodily form and manage an individual's mental traits. There are seven focus chakras: four in the chest, which regulate cerebral traits, and three in the lower, which control instinctive properties. **They are arranged vertically along the spine:**

1. Muladhara Chakra (Root Chakra)
2. Svadhishthana (Sacral Chakra) is the second chakra.
3. Manipura (Solar Plexus Chakra) is the third chakra.
4. Anahata (Chakra of the Heart)
5. Vishuddha (Throat Chakra) is the fifth chakra.
6. Ajna (Three-Eye Chakra)
7. Sahasrara Chakra (Crown Chakra)

Many individuals believe that their chakras are either obstructed or not functioning properly. Harmony with oneself is impossible to achieve until the chakras are adjusted. Genuine happiness becomes ambiguous. This is the moment at which the chakras must be opened. This should be feasible by employing mudras, which are unusual hand positions that may transport greater vitality to certain chakras. Some specific sounds are also recited to enhance the impact of mudras. They generate a reverberation in the body when spoken, which may be felt in the chakra for which they are indicated.

•Root Chakra

This chakra is located at the base of the spine and represents one's foundation and sense of being grounded. It is about endurance difficulties like money and nutrition.

Instructions for activating the Root Chakra:

•Predict a standard contemplative position.

•Allow the tips of your thumb and pointer to make delicate contact in a calm movement.

•Currently, concentrate on the Root chakra.

•Serenade the sound "LAM" softly yet clearly.

•Continue to take deep breaths until you are completely relaxed.

2. The Sacral Chakra

This chakra is located towards the lower abdomen, around two crawls under the navel (or the width of three fingers). It is about feelings of prosperity, sexuality, and pleasure.

Methods for Activating the Sacral Chakra:

•Accept a simple contemplating act.

•Place the left hand underneath the right hand, with the left palm touching the

proper hand's rear fingers.

•Allow the tips of the thumbs to make delicate contact.

•Currently, concentrate on the Sacral chakra.

•Serenade the sound "VAM" quietly till you are completely relaxed.

3. The Chakra of the Solar Plexus

This chakra is located above the stomach in the upper belly. It is about feelings of

self-esteem, self-assurance, and confidence.

•Take a standard meditation stance.

•Place your hands in front of your tummy, just under your Solar Plexus.

•Allow your fingers to connect at their tips, all pointing infinitely away from you.

•Cross your thumbs and fix different fingers.

•Currently, concentrate on the Solar Plexus chakra.

•Serenade the sound "Smash" quietly yet clearly till you are completely unfastened

.

4. The heart chakra.

This chakra represents one's ability to experience, give, and receive love. When obstructed, love, pleasure, and internal harmony may suffer.

•Accept the standard contemplative stance.

•Allow your pointer and thumb tips to address two hands.

•Place your left hand on your left thigh.

•Place your right hand in front of the bottom half of your breastbone.

•Currently, concentrate on the Heart chakra, which is located simply over the heart.

•Serenade the sound "YAM" quietly and simply for around 10 minutes.

•A comprehensive and sophisticated view of the chakras.

5: Chakra is the Throat Chakra.

This chakra is located in the neck and is concerned with communication, self-expression, emotions, and reality.

•Accept the standard contemplative stance.

•Cross your fingers in your hands, except the thumbs.

•Allow the thumbs to make contact at their tips and point up.

•Currently, concentrate on the Throat Chakra, which is located at the base of the throat.

•Serenade the sound "HAM" quietly, yet unmistakably. Continue reciting for

5 to 10 minutes.

6. The Chakra of the Third Eye

This chakra is located in the temple's core and is concerned with one's ability to concentrate and perceive the 10,000-foot vista. It is about instinct, the creative mind, intellect, and the ability to make decisions.

•Accept the standard pondering act.

•Place your hands in front of the bottom half of the sternum.

•Keep your middle fingers straight, connecting their points and pointing away from your body indefinitely.

•Maintain different fingers twisted and in contact at the upper two pha-langes.

•The tips of your thumbs should emphasize you and make touch with you.

•Currently, concentrate on the Third-Eye chakra, which is located slightly above

the focal point of the two brows.

●Serenade the sound "OM" quietly, yet clearly.

●Continue to recite till your feelings are reinforced.

7. The Crown Chakra

This chakra is located at the crown of the head and is concerned with inside and outward perfection, one's relationship with the 'Soul,' and pure bliss. It is the highest chakra.

●Accept the standard reflection stance.

●Place your hands in front of your stomach.

●Allow your ring fingers to face up and make contact at their tips.

●Keep your remaining fingers crossed, with your left thumb below your right.

●Now, concentrate on the Crown chakra, which is located at the crown of your head.

●Serenade the sound "NG" quietly for around 10 minutes.

Make certain you serenade it.

You should be prospering comparatively; you are merely trudging through life and feel far from your optimal level. Perhaps you are exhausted or overworked. You may be dealing with physical medical issues or committed struggles. Your chakras are most likely obstructed. Your body's vitality is not flowing properly, causing a variety of issues. By using nine easy steps, you can avoid stress. However, by using incredible strategies to open and balance your chakras, you can reclaim essentialness, vitality, harmony, clarity, well-being, and joy in your life.

Which Chakras Do You Have?

Your chakras are the points in your body where life energy flows. When one or more of your chakras get blocked, it creates an imbalance and a lack of free flow in your framework, which may lead to physical, emotional, and serious medical issues.

Your root chakra is located at the base of your spine, near your tailbone. It refers to the idea of being anchored as well as endurance difficulties such as nutrition and money. Your sacral chakra is located in your lower midregion. It refers to your affiliation and ability to recognize new encounters and individuals around you, as well as your success, sexuality, pleasure, and plenty.

Your solar plexus chakra is located in your upper midriff. It is associated with your self-esteem, confidence, and certainty. Your heart chakra is located in the center of your chest. It refers to your ability for adoration, inner harmony, and joy. Your throat chakra is located in your throat region. It is associated with your ability to communicate and self-articulate your feelings. Your third eye is located on your temple, between your eyes. It refers to your ability to center, instinct, creative mind, ability to grasp the big picture, acumen, and ability to make big decisions. Your crown chakra is the most important chakra in your body, located at the top of your head. It is associated with your ability to be entirely connected deeply and experience an absolute joy.

Are Chakras a Real Thing?

Chakras were initially portrayed in the Vedas quite some time ago. Individuals have benefited from chakra-balancing practices since that time and for all time. In any event, your chakras are not responsible for your organs. They are not fixed and obvious things that can be contacted and examined by specialists. So, would they say they've been experimentally proven? At this moment, chakras have not been rationally proven. However, the vitality that exists within you has not.

Regardless, the idea that "everything is vitality" is a deductively demonstrated reality widely accepted in quantum material science. The chakra hypothesis and chakra-adjusting systems are based on the idea of ever-flowing vitality. Konstantin Korotkov of St. Petersburg Federal University of Informational Technologies used the possibility of Chinese meridians in the mid-1990s to build up a logical gadget called GDV that can quantify bio-vitality in your body by taking note of vitality points that relate to prosperity and various elements of the body. There have also been several studies on how elevating your consciousness and activities like yoga, introspection, reiki, gratitude, and using jewels may open up your chakras to benefit your physical and emotional welfare. Regardless of whether you believe in chakras completely, are skeptical, or fall somewhere in the center, your well-being and prosperity might benefit from chakra-opening exercises.

You should try these techniques if you need more equalization, internal harmony, wellness, and pleasure in your life.

9 Ways to Activate Your Chakras

Meditation:

Contemplation is a novel way to connect with your soul and seek guidance from your higher self. It is an excellent method for staying in the present moment, releasing negative or trapped energy and unfavorable obstructions, welcoming fresh and good vitality, and adjusting your chakras. While any type of reflection is beneficial for opening up your chakras, explicitly guided contemplations to enact your chakras are the most effective.

Yoga:

Yoga is a fantastic way to open up and balance your chakras by opening up your body. Different positions offer different benefits. The camel post, for example, may balance your heart and throat chakras at the same time. A simple yoga practice may help you rebalance your mind, body, and spirit. TaiChi and QiGong are relatively beneficial practices for opening your chakras and balancing your energies.

Mantras and Affirmations:

Mantras are a fantastic way to open oneself up to infinite love and empathy. You may use them during introspection or when summarizing them for anybody to hear or in your mind.

You might use Sanskrit words or consider your mantras. Positive confirmations, like mantras, may develop positive energy in your body. Use the assertions that you need the most. You may summarize your confirmations in your head or even record them for everyone to hear.

The most impressive aspect is the combination of everything.

Innovative Visualization:

An innovative perception is a fantastic tool for clearing your mind of negative chatter. Put oneself in a relaxed condition by sitting on a cushion, sleeping on a comfortable bed, or even better, lying on some green grass in nature. Consider images and colors that speak to you about love and fulfillment. Carry yourself to a happy place. Consider a heart or a blossom opening for each of your chakras.

Deep Breathing:

When you're done with probabilities, deep and deliberate breaths might help you re-establish your chakras. Each inhalation gives life to each chakra, while each exhalation allows attention to sink into your chakras. This exercise may open up your chakras and restore harmony to your brain, body, and soul.

Absolution:

Holding onto sentiments of wrath, indignation, lament, and sadness and refusing to let go of past wrongs may generate a slew of obstructions in your ever-flowing energy, particularly in your heart chakra.

Pardon. Don't give up. Journaling, rituals, a good cry, growth, time in nature, introspection, and yoga may all help you get back on track. Seeking competent guidance from an advocate or mentor may also be beneficial. Keep in mind that closing one component allows another to open up.

Gratitude:

Practicing gratitude will instantly improve your energy and awaken your chakras. A practice of gratitude may attract more riches, pleasure, well-being, harmony, love, crucial relationships, and other wonderful qualities into your life. After you wake up, think about all the things you are grateful for in your life. Keep a gratitude journal and write down at least three things you were glad for that day each night. Discover a duty for gratitude and share your daily admiration with one another.

Take a few moments during the day to be grateful for the simple things.

Colors:

Each of your chakras corresponds to a different frequency and emits a different color. The root chakra is red, the sacral chakra is orange, the sun-oriented plexus is yellow, the heart chakra is green, the throat chakra is blue, the third eye is indigo, and the crown chakra is violet. Wearing appropriate hues, chakra-shaded arm jewelry, consuming brilliant candles (e.g., green candles for your heart chakra), or lying beneath a Chacrys precious stone bed that uses hued chakra lights will help you change your chakras.

Precious stones:

Precious stones and gemstones are an easy and consistent way to open your chakras, activate the natural evolution of energy inside you, and balance your brain, body, and soul. Amethysts are excellent for the crown chakra, sodalite for the third eye, chrysocolla for the throat chakra, rose quartz for the heart chakra, citrine for the sun-powered plexus, carnelian for the sacral chakra, and hematite for the root chakra.

Vogel stones are an excellent choice if you are looking for a valuable stone that can benefit all of your chakras while also modifying your whole body, mind, and soul. Vogel precious stones are pure, common stone gems that may re-establish, govern, and balance the vitality flow in your body, assisting you to revitalize and heal.

Activity: Determine which kind of training benefits or affects you: physical or reflective? Would you be able to set aside some time to concentrate and think, or would you want to schedule a one-hour recovery meeting?

Activity: Check out the list of 7 chakras and related sites to get acquainted with precise methods for opening each particular chakra.

CHAPITRE 9: LET'S DISCUSS MYTHS

Kundalini, the serpent force that activates the chakras, has become a prominent topic in new-age thought, alternative medicine, and yoga. In any event, there is a growing gap between how the chakras are seen now and how they are valued in traditional yogic discourse. Today, the chakras are primarily used for physical recuperation. This is a one-of-a-kind and best-case scenario introduction to the yogic practice of self-awareness, which is concerned with getting beyond the body and brain. Opening the chakras requires a drastic shift in consciousness, which usually occurs after a long period of contemplation. It's not primarily an issue of impassioned openness or bodily purification.

Today, the chakras, like yoga, are defined in concrete terms, which obscures their true reason and capacity.

What has happened to the chakras is comparable to what has happened to yoga. Yoga requires contemplation, which is defined as "the abolition of the dualistic ways of thinking of the brain" (Yoga Sutra 1.2).

Regardless, today, yoga has come to mean fundamentally asana (yogic stances), which is just a guide to achieving yoga. Chakra (not "shakra" as many people say) is a Sanskrit word that means "wheel," or "that which rotates." It refers to the seven basic communities in the rational or astral body, the group of life energy important to the physical body, in yogic literature.

Their beginning takes into account the unfolding of higher states of cognizance, prompting the consciousness of the Supreme Self. However, the chakras, like yoga, are now characterized in real terms, which obscures their true reason and capacity.

"The subject of chakras will not be simple," Swami Satyananda wrote in Kundalini Tantra. Perhaps he assumed it was a topic unfamiliar to his audience, or perhaps he simply assumed the question wasn't simple. The issue of chakras is fascinating to us in the modern world for two reasons. Our initial handle of a difficult topic is fundamentally a simplified one, but if we're not careful, our first handle may be our lone handle. Have we mistakenly corrupted a complex collection of knowledge embedded in a profoundly unique culture and language?

Most yoga students are familiar with the concept of chakras.

Misguided Belief #1: How to Express "Chakra"

Do you remember this tongue twister? "How much wood could a woodchuck throw if he could throw wood?" Say, "Toss, toss, toss."

Throw in "ra" and you get "toss ra." In the official Sanskrit transcription, "c" is articulated as "ch" as in "chapel," therefore you may see "chakra" as well as "chakra." Remember the woodchuck, whichever it is spelled.

Misguided Judgment #2: The Chakras are "things" that live in the body, maybe in the nerve plexuses, organs, or the spine...

It goes without saying that the chakras are not physical entities. However, those of us who are vehemently opposed may not have given this enough thought. We keep talking as if a post-mortem examination would reveal a string of various colored lotuses running through the center of the middle, or as if a chakra is just another organ like the liver or the spleen. Consider a chakra to be a point of convergence for major vitality channels (Nadis) on a plane of awareness, bringing in psycho-substantial encounters and abilities and serving as a point of convergence for reflection and otherworldly exercise.

Here are some relevant definitions:

1. Awareness vortex in the body.
2. A focus on representation in the yogic body.

3. Calculation based on phenomenology.

Misconception #3: The Chakras are enticing shades of the rainbow!

However, there is no mention of rainbows in the source writings. Various writings depict various hues (or, more often than not, no shading at all). The navel location lotus, for example, maybe black, dim green, dim blue, dazzling, or red.

Partnering the chakras with colors is a perceptual technique, not a representation of physical reality.

Another difficulty with the notion of chakras having specific colors, as shown in the Shat-Chakra-Nirupana Tantra right now: The adhara lotus (Muladhara chakra) is made up of four blood-red petals with gold Sanskrit characters, a yellow pericarp, and a crimson Dakini Devi. The svadhishthana chakra has a vermilion lotus and the color of lightning. Its god, Hari, is blue but dressed in yellow, and the Devi Rakini, who is also blue, sits on a red lotus in the radiantly white pericarp. The Manipura lotus is the color of a rain cloud, with blue letters and a red pericarp. Its deity, Rudra, is red but seems white due to residuals, while the Shakti Lakini is blue and rests on a red lotus.

What exactly is shading?

Partnering the chakras with colors is part of a perceptive technique that, as it turns out, fluctuates according to tradition. Depictions are for training with a particular objective or result in mind, not to depict reality in the physical world.

The five components (bhutas) are an often-used approach for dealing with chakras. The geometric form and color of each of the five bhutas are built up in five chakras, which are generally associated with the pelvic floor, pelvis, navel, heart, and throat.

Color and Shape of Bhuta Chakra and Body Associations That Are Common:
Muladhara > Prithvi > Yellow Square > Pelvic Floor
Svadishthana > genital area, lower belly > Apas (water)
Manipura > Agni (fire) > Manipura > Navel Zone
Vayu (air) > dim blue hexagram > Anahata > chest, heart focus point

Space > blackish circle > vishuddha > throat

Regardless, even this affiliation shifts.

For example, the Goraksha-Paddhati depicts a training for focusing on the earth component as a yellow square at the heart place, the water component as a white half-moon structure at the throat, the fire component as a triangle at the sense of taste, the air component between the brows, and the space component at the Brahmarandhra (the opening to brahman—all-encompassing cognizance—experienced at or over the crown of the head).

Misunderstanding #4: There are seven chakras.

I have a lovely illustration from Nath Charit that depicts 12 chakras, four of them between the two-petaled lotus at the brow community and the significant petaled lotus above the top of the head. Gorakshanatha's Siddha-Siddhanta-Paddhati portrays nine chakras. The Netra Tan six (pelvic floor, navel, heart, sense of taste, eyebrow, and crown), all have unusual names compared to the most well-known framework today.

Abhinavagupta, a well-known Kashmiri tantric expert, illustrates a five-chakra structure: the base, Kanda (pelvis), the heart, the sense of taste, and the crown. A prominent Shaiva material, the Vijnana Bhairava Tantra, also alludes to 12 chakras.

The current 6 + 1 framework (root, pelvis, navel, heart, throat, and brow focus, in addition to one over the highest point of the head) is just one of many frameworks that show 3, 4, 5, 9, 11, or 12 main focuses. There are several vitality habitats, as well as 12 important focal points within the body's center pivot. Minor vitality habitats are called marma focuses in Ayurveda, and concentrations adjusted along the axis of the body are called chakras. Why are there so many different frameworks?

The number of points recorded and shown is determined by the training or habit. Various schools of thought or messages employ a different calculated model to recommend or depict representations, practices, and summons of forces (divinities). For example, some cultures stress the Talu chakra, which governs the sensitive sense of taste, whilst others do not. A few traditions have elaborated practices for at least six chakras; others concentrate solely around the navel or pelvis, with the heart and cerebrum as focal points.

The reality behind the unassuming body is much vaster and more mysterious than we realize.

Mistake #5: The second chakra is all about sex.

To be honest, there are a plethora of desires that arise as a result of nature, karma, and the innate need to be alive, connect, and improve both communal experience (bhoga) and extreme opportunity (apavarga). Instead of seeing explicit desires as chakra-specific, it is wiser to seek/desire our inborn richness as humans and the establishment of life in the body. And after that, keep in mind that although all schools of yoga encourage fantastic quality, transformation, or supremacy of various arousing desires, they differ in how that greatness is to occur.

MISTAKES ABOUT CHAKRA YOGA AND HEALING:

In most New Age thought, imbalanced chakra features or blocks are considered the foundation of infection, which is subsequently addressed by altering the capability of the impacted chakra. This misunderstanding has resulted in a slew of specialists promising to restore our chakras for us.

Others claim to be able to activate our chakras and so repair what bothers us, as well as provide us with private knowledge and experience. A part of these systems may be costly, and many are very theoretical.

Most chakra healing nowadays emphasizes exterior estimations, for example, pearls, herbs, massage, sound or shading therapy, and vibrational mending; various equipment is often used to treat the chakras. Furthermore, clairvoyant healers guarantee that their psychological or mysterious forces will legitimately chip away at the chakras.

Using such tactics to open or agitate the chakras should result in greater levels of cognition in the person being treated.

The yogic approach is intended to open the chakras, not for recuperation or to increase mystery powers, but rather as part of the process of Self-information. For this yoga, we must do internal actions such as mantra, pranayama, and introspection; external approaches such as nutrition or medicines are only supplementary guides.

According to the yoga theory, the chakras are closed; that is, they don't actually operate, in the typical human condition, which is occasionally elevated beyond only via thorough supportive practice. The result is not an infection, but rather obliviousness. This numbness is defined by considering the outer world as the true truth and living without acquaintance with one's true self, which is neither body nor mind; nonetheless, awareness is achieved without cognition. One's chakras may be closed, yet one can still be healthy, well-adjusted, intellectually imaginative, and productive in a variety of daily situations. The purpose of opening the chakras is not to better one's capacity in the typical areas of human existence, but to transcend our human and fleeting gazing to the godlike embodiment.

The chakras are not part of the normal operation of the physical body. They play an important role only when there is heightened consciousness or intense arousal. They refer to the opening up or emerging of the inconspicuous body with consciousness beyond it. While we can relate physical and inconspicuous body parts and capacities, we must recognize that the two are not the same, and the profoundly opened astral or unobtrusive body is something entirely different.

KUNDALINI:

If the chakras are to function properly, they need a more powerful source of energy than the human body can provide. This is the function of the kundalini, or serpent force, which is dormant in the human body. Kundalini is neither physical strength nor vitality that can be controlled with individual effort. Kundalini is the focused energy of attention or thoughtfulness. It is not a vitality detached from cognizance, but rather the vitality that manifests with consciousness when it is released from thinking. Only if a person has one-sharpness of the mind can kundalini really arrive energetically, since only then does one have the possibility of going beyond notions.

Kundalini activation necessitates the entry of prana, or life force, into the Sushumna, or focal channel. This occurs when the prana is drawn back from its fixation by the way one thinks about the outside world. For as long as our life energy remains associated with the physical body and its powers, it cannot be drawn back into the focal channel. Thus, awakening the kundalini and opening the chakras includes a state of samadhi in which we lose common cognizance. At first, this usually involves a state of stupor in which we become oblivious to our physical bodies. Later, it is done in the waking state, with no impediment to physical activity; also, at that organization, the physical body is never again perceived as one's genuine character.

The chakras may be named after the elements they govern in a more exact though fundamental way.

THE PHYSICAL ORGANS AND THE CHAKRAS:

Because the Sanskrit expressions for the chakras are cumbersome, they have been named after their corresponding physical area: Crown chakra, forehead chakra, throat chakra, heart chakra, navel chakra, sex chakra, and root chakra are the seven chakras. While this is beneficial, it also increases the likelihood of mistaking the chakras for the physical body. The chakras are named for the components they govern: earth for the base of the spine, water for the urogenital region, fire for the navel, air for the heart, ether for the neck, mind for the third eye, and cognition for the crown chakra.

Regardless, it is the grandiose aspects of these components that the opened chakras provide access to, not their regular roles as parts of our own reality. The opened chakras provide knowledge about the unity of the universe's target constituents (components), as well as the instruments of understanding (sense organs) and the instruments of action (organs of activity), which are the universe's emotional constituents. When we open the chakras, we experience the infinite idea of these components within our own further mindfulness.

The gross or physical focus must be put in a state of rest or equilibrium in order to bring the inconspicuous focus into operation. That is why yoga practices (asana, pranayama, pratyahara, and Dharana) promote calm of the body, breath, senses, and mind. To properly activate the water chakra, for example, is not the same as having heightened sexual desire. Actually, it necessitates that the physical, sexual organ be rendered inactive and that the sexual drive be sublimated.

Thus, opening the air chakra is distinct from feeling uplifted, powerless, or overly enthusiastic. To activate this fourth chakra, we must look beyond tiny individual sentiments and see the immense life underlying every single ecstatic shift. This necessitates an opening to extensive feelings of empathy and commitment, as well as interaction with the all-encompassing life force.

As a result, there is no such chakra as the sex chakra, the heart chakra, or any other chakra as a minor bodily function. There is a chakra in the unpretentious body in a territory that corresponds to a region of the sex organs in the physical body, and it has an unnoticeable companion. However, the appropriately opened chakra isn't concerned with the elements of the physical, and sexual organs, but rather with the infinite component of water and its contrasting exercises. Consider this: a sex community thrives on misunderstanding.

The signs of open chakras include a sense of command over and detachment from bodily components and organs. Up to one is linked to the physical organs and their powers, and the inconspicuous organs cannot potentially become the most significant aspect. The enlivening of the mind behind the unpretentious body involves the ability to remove the gross body and its capabilities, such as a heavy jacket, which is never again required on a hot summer day.

INDICATIONS OF CHAKRA OPENING:

To get a sense of what occurs as the chakras open, let us examine the indicators of opening, chakra by chakra. Please keep in mind that these are generic indicators. Experience varies, particularly when it comes to miracles or abilities. The primary sensation is an expanding sense of the universe's solidarity with one's own Self-nature.

Let us examine the signs of opening chakra by chakra.

EARTH CHAKRA:

When the first chakra is opened, one becomes aware of the vast earth component and conscious of the fundamental solidarity of every single powerful condition of a problem as a crystallization of the energy of awareness. The qualities of the astronomical earth component, such as hardness, unpleasantness, thickness, and surface, are encountered as varied vibratory states of one's own consciousness. A variety of inconspicuous or wonderful fragrances may be detected.

Every single developmental act known to man may be seen as varied actions of the immense earth's vitality in its power to form and sustain the structure.

WATER CHAKRA:

When the water chakra is awakened, one becomes aware of the magnificent water component and aware of the fundamental unity of every fluid situation of the problem as a crystallization of the life of consciousness. As different vibratory states of one's own awareness, one comes to encounter water component characteristics such as delicate quality, wetness, coolness, and streaming nature. Different inconspicuous or divine tastes can be seen as a pith (rasa) that emanates from all encounters. Thus, all known pacificator demonstrations are seen as various activities of the astronomical water vitality in its pacificator role.

FIRE CHAKRA:

When the third chakra is opened, one becomes aware of the tremendous fire component and conscious of the essential unity of every bright state of the problem as a crystallization of the life of consciousness. The properties of the fire component, such as light, shade, warmth, and enlightenment, are encountered as distinct vibratory levels of one's own consciousness.

Unpretentious visions and dreams may also be encountered, and the brightness or mood underlying things can be seen. Essentially, one comprehends the operations of the enormous fire vitality in its capacity of illumination underlying all appearances known to humans.

AIR CHAKRA:

When the fourth chakra is opened, one becomes aware of the endless air component and aware of the fundamental unity of every vaporous situation of an issue as a crystallization of the life of awareness. The qualities of the air component, such as movement, diversity, subtlety, and infiltration, are encountered as varied vibratory states of one's own consciousness. Inconspicuous vitality interactions may also be seen, and the latent vibratory impulses of the tremendous life power can be felt. Similarly, one comprehends the roles of the large air vigor in its enabling job behind all interactions known to man.

ETHER CHAKRA:

When the fifth Chakra is awakened, one becomes aware of the magnificent ether component and cognizant of the essential unity of all space known to man as a crystallization of the energy of awareness. The features of a space, such as delicacy, subtlety, inescapability, and clarity, are encountered as distinct vibratory levels of one's own consciousness. Unobtrusive noises and the universe's secret spatial structure may also be perceived.

Similarly, one understands the workings of the incomparable ether component as their grid behind all vibrations known to man.

BRAIN CHAKRA OR THIRD EYE:

When the sixth chakra is opened, one becomes aware of the grandiose brain and conscious of the essential solidarity of all personalities known to humanity as a crystallization of the energy of awareness. The psyche's traits, such as perceptiveness, imagination, separation, and detachment, are encountered as distinct vibratory states of one's own awareness. Through the movement of the stirred brain, one gains the ability to incorporate all of the vast components and their individual organs and capacities. One gains power over the mind and develops a never-ending recognition of observations. One realizes that whatever we think is evidence of the psyche's astronomical reign.

AWARENESS CHAKRA:

When the seventh chakra opens, one becomes aware of the self or pure awareness as the solitary reality and hidden essence of the cosmos. As one's own inclination and the basic idea of the universe, one encounters cognizance characteristics such as interminability, eternal status, harmony, and joy. One gains supremacy over consciousness and comes to dwell in the realm of Self-awareness, perceiving oneself in all animals and all creatures in oneself. Everything is understood to be manifestations of the Supreme Self, which is the only reality.

There are also wide indicators of the enlivening of inconspicuous energies and resources, such as the meeting of unobtrusive noises, lights, deity dreams, and so on, mostly in the third eye region. Such experiences, however, may occur before a certain chakra is awakened.

EXPERIENCES AND POWERS OF THE CLAIRVOYANT:

Each chakra may focus on comparing layers of the cosmos or other realms beyond the physical. The corresponding sub-planes of the astral realm, which are much more dazzling than anything in the physical world, may become available for human exploration. We may get a comparison understanding of nature's unadorned operations, abilities, existing power, and the technique of grandiose creation and control over them.

Each chakra may provide an awareness of comparing cosmos levels or other realms beyond the physical.

However, not all yogis choose to research the universes or the resources associated with the chakras. Many extraordinary jnanis or yogis of the way of knowledge endeavor to legitimately combine into unadulterated solidarity or the Absolute. They may hardly notice the qualities and capabilities of the chakras as they enliven. Ramana Maharshi personifies this viewpoint.

For him, there was just one chakra or center, the Self, from which all the marvels of the coarse and inconspicuous worlds and bodies appeared like mirror images or air pockets on the floods of the ocean.

CHAPITRE 10: YOU AND YOUR NADIS

According to traditional Eastern wellness sciences, for example, Ayurveda and yoga reasoning, every living thing has the ability to function because of the existence of vitality known as prana, which travels through the body via the unadorned routes known as nadis. Only when the nadis are clean and the firm can prana flow.

When the Nadi framework is obstructed, prana cannot flow and an individual's physical and psychological well-being suffers.

The three major Nadis are as follows:

nadi ida - Ida nadi, or the left channel, originates in the Muladhara (root) chakra and flows to one side, zigzagging all the way around the chakras until ending in the left nostril. This Nadi represents mental vigor.

Pingala nadi - Also known as the proper channel, Pingala nadi starts at the root chakra but flows to one side, zigzagging all through the chakras in the same manner as ida nadi and ending with the correct nostril. Pingala nadi is the source of prana.

Sushumna nadi - The focusing channel goes straight up the spine and through the chakras, from just under the root chakra to the Sahasrara (crown) chakra. This is the Nadi of extraterrestrial mindfulness.

One of the most important aspects of Hatha yoga is altering the Nadis, and one of the greatest strategies for doing so is a sort of pranayama known as Nadi shodhana or alternate nostril relaxation. It is often added towards the end of asana practice.

The Nadis are similar to the meridians used in Chinese needle treatment.

NDS are vitality conduits that carry PRNA - divine vitality, life, and awareness - via them. There is an inconspicuous and perfect system of 72,000 Nādīs within the human body that conveys this vital force throughout the whole body. The Nādīs are related to the sensory system on the physical level. Their influence, however, extends beyond this to the astral and profound planes of our reality. If all of the Nādīs are functioning properly, we are safe and, for the most part, joyful. Nonetheless, almost all of us have some physical or clairvoyant issue, implying that a portion of the Nādīs is not functioning properly and should be adjusted. I PRNA is conscious vitality, which means that the Nādīs also transfer awareness. Methods for the Nādīs allow one to see and hear things across a wide range and move in varied degrees of awareness.

There have been several tales of people who were clinically dead and then came back to life. They almost completely represented how they moved down a corridor with light issuing at the end.

This is the Nd via which the body's life leaves.

Such "burrow encounters" might also occur in our dreams and during astral travel. With them, we are not so much beyond the body as we are in a different state of consciousness. The Nādīs enable us to go on mental journeys of revelation across the whole Universe. Our consciousness may go anywhere we desire with their help without the body moving in any way.

IDĀ, PINGALĀ and SUSHUMNĀ are three Nādīs of unusual importance.

1. ID appears on the left side of the body and communicates with the moon's guidelines.
2. PINGAL begins on the proper side of the body and represents the sun's guideline.
3. SUSHUMN communicates with awareness via the focal channel of the spinal rope.

PINGAL has a partner in the Parasympathetic Nervous System, ID in the

Sympathetic Nervous System, and SUSHUMN in the Central Nervous System.

The moon represents the brain with its fluctuating emotions, whilst the sun represents astuteness. Similarly, just as our emotions and thoughts change all the time, so does the moon's structure. However, the mind, like the sun, is a fixed and consistent guideline. We are sound and suitable for future intellectual and deep growth only when agreement and equalization prevail between the moon framework and the sun framework.

Through the breath, we can enact and fit the Nādīs. When we breathe in through the left nostril in Prnyma, we activate the Id Nd. The Id Nd, like the moonlight, cools, quietens, and revitalizes the body and mind. Pingal Nd, on the other hand, which is influenced by breathing via the proper nostril, has a warming and enacting effect, similar to how sunshine warms the land and animates the growth of flora.

Id and Pingal begin in the cerebrum around the level of the Pituitary Gland. Pingal affects the left side of the equator, while Id affects the right side. To maintain balance, both Nādīs run in a snake-like pattern from one side of the body to the other. They also meet the focal Nd, Sushumn, at the points where they intersect. Where the force and brilliance of the sun and moon meet, along with the reinforcing impact of the Sushumn, exceptionally incredible vitality communities known as the CHAKRAS structure are formed.

The Throat Chakra (Vishuddhi Chakra) is shaped by the main junction of the Nādīs at the highest point of the spinal segment, while the Root Center (Mūlādhāra Chakra) is framed by the final intersection at the base of the spinal section. The Id Nd flows on the left half of the body and the Pingal Nd on the right, and it is precisely here where our sluggish consciousness is hidden.

The Nādīs form a type of bunch (GRANTHI) at a few points along the spinal section, each of which marks a significant moment in our deep development. When these clusters are "loosened," the vitality contained within them is activated, and the hidden forces (SIDDHIS) have given us recuperating powers, the seeing of past and future, the seeing of airs, and otherworldly capacities.

GANG, YAMUN, and SARASVAT are different expressions for Id, Pingal, and Sushumn. They are the names of India's three holiest rivers. Gang and Yamun flow on the surface, whereas Sarasvati flows underneath. It rises to the surface just once, like clockwork. This occurrence is associated with a certain planetary celestial body and is known as the KUMBHA MEL. This spectacular otherworldly festival of India, celebrated at the confluence of these three streams (Sangam), is attended by a large number of people who come to achieve liberation from their Karmas and the cycle of resurrection by bathing in the sacred waters. In any event, the three essential Nādīs are the "divine waterways" for the Yogi, and the gy Chakra (the brow community) where these Nādīs meet is the auspicious location of a trip where the Yogi obtains freedom.

Similarly, to the mysterious Sarasvat, which only appears on rare occasions, the Sushumn Nd is only dynamic for brief periods of time (for example, at first light and sunset). When the three basic Nādīs merge into one continuous flow stream - the deep vitality of the Sushumna Nādīs. The vitality also flows via this Nd in deep thought and in Samdh. We are tortured by constantly shifting CHITTA VRITTIS - contemplations, sensations, worries, and so forth - for however long the Sushumna remains inactive. However, when the Sushumna begins to flow, the influxes of the brain cease and we "wash" in the rapture of celestial cognizance.

If you have a basic understanding of kundalini yoga, you may have come across the terms 'Chakras' and 'Nadis'. What are they, and how will they affect you and how you live your life? They have a huge effect!

Chakras are active centers where Ida and Pingala (manly and ladylike energies) meet and merge to form Sushumna. More information on the Chakras can be found here. In Sanskrit, the name 'Chakra' means 'Wheel' or 'Turning Disk'. It gets its name from the nature and growth of the vitality that dwells along the spinal cord of the body.

There are about 108 chakras located throughout the body.

In any case, the major seven along the spine are the main ones we allude to, being the enormous axles of vitality. Numerous Tantric writings state that the human body contains 72,000 nadis that channel prana to each cell. What exactly are Nadis? The vitality conduits through which the energies of the physical, unobtrusive, and causal bodies circulate are known as nadis. The seven chakras are formed by the gathering or association of both Ida and

Pingala Nadis.

Ida Nadi's bio:

Ida, associated with the vigor of the moon, refers to the ladylike aspect of our personality and is typically shown as white. It is also known as the Yin component in Chinese thought. Ida is in charge of the parasympathetic sensory system, which calms the brain and body since it is associated with sensations, emotions, and memories.

When Ida becomes too solid or dominant, fatigue, despair, self-preoccupation, and the inability to perceive things from a rational perspective might take over.

The Ida Nadi is aloof, remote, and feminine in the yogic tradition, where it is called the moon Nadi (Chandra Nadi). In many circumstances, the yogic grouping of Chandra Namaskar is practiced throughout the full moon's seven-day stretch to re-establish and recharge the Ida Nadi channel.

Pingala Nadi's bio:

While Pingala, associated with the vitality of the sun, speaks to the manly side of our nature and is frequently depicted as red. It directs the cognitive sensory system and animates physical and mental activity. Pingala Nadi is responsible for justifiable, rational, and explanatory zeal. Pingala is also a Yang component in the Chinese way of thinking. Pingala Nadi, also known as the Sun Nadi (Surya Nadi) in the yogic tradition, is lively, extroverted, and masculine. In many circumstances, the yoga sequence of Surya Namaskar is practiced in the morning or when the sun is rising to gather dynamic energy to bolster the Pingala Nadi channel.

Shushumna Nadi's bio:

Ida and Pingala begin and terminate on opposite sides of the Sushumna, traveling in spirals like the DNA helix, intersecting at each chakra or vitality portal.

Sushumna is the energy line that goes from the base of the spine to the top of the head and transfers Kundalini vitality, the underlying transformational force inside, upwards as it is awakened by the act of Yoga and contemplation.

Sushumna Nadi is the spiritual channel that should be focused on. It requires getting to the focal point of the spinal line and balancing both Ida and Pingala Nadis.

Sushumna Nadi may open and flow uninhibitedly when Ida and Pingala Nadis are adjusted and clean; hence, sanitization of all three nadis is critical for overall well-being, body and psyche health, and deep growth.

Concerning Kundalini:

Kundalini is a Sanskrit term from ancient India that denotes the emergence of imaginative vitality power (also known as sexual vitality) and awareness, which has been snaked at the base of the spine since birth and is the source of existing power (pranic vitality, chi, bio-vitality). It refers to a form of basic life (or shakti) in Hinduism. Kundalini arousal is thought to occur as a result of intense meditation, which sometimes results in feelings of enlightenment and joy. Kundalini arousals, on the other hand, may happen in a variety of ways.

Numerous yoga frameworks revolve around awakening Kundalini through reflection, pranayama breathing, asana practice, and mantra recitation. As a result, unless stimulated by these activities and otherworldly experiences, Kundalini's vigor remains dormant or resting inside the body.

The Breath and Its Relationship:

Consideration of mind on the advancement of breath at the nostrils is one of the most immediate strategies for modifying energies and causing prana to flow in Sushumna. It will bite by bit open by taking care of the smaller flowing nostril. By looking after each other, the two of them will flow more freely. Sushumna's calm gradually awakens when both are treated as one constant stream. While this training may appear to be simple, it necessitates delicate perseverance and the ability to concentrate. As a result, the nadis current may be monitored by controlling and redirecting breath.

Rearranged, this may be seen as the breath being a 'force' that ousts or drives out vitality, whilst breath maintenance (holding and developing) can assist apply the balance in the Nadi that is unbalanced or lethargic/inert.

CHAPTER 11: HISTORY

Now that the chakras have become New Age jargon, there are numerous interpretations of their significance and potential floating about. While the chakras are becoming a household term, they are also disseminating a great deal of perplexing, contradictory, and frequently incorrect data. It is critical to recognize that the chakras are based on an ancient tradition that many New Age teachers have hardly examined. Here's a quick breakdown of how the chakras is improving in general.

The Vedas are India's most established composed convention (1,500 - 500 BC), written from oral custom by higher-level Brahmins, who may have descended from the Aryan stock that reached India from the north. The initial meaning of the term chakra as "wheel" refers to the chariot wheels of the monarchs, known as chakravartin. (The correct spelling, however, is cakra, articulated with a ch as in the chapel.) The term was also a metaphor for the sun, which "crosses the world like the triumphant chariot of a chakravartin and represents the eternal wheel of time known as the Kalachakra, which speaks to divine request and equalization."

The appearance of a chakravartin was thought to herald a new age, and they were pictured as being preceded by a bright plate of light, much like the glory of Christ, with just this spinning circle located before them (perhaps their astounding third chakras). It is also stated that the deity Vishnu fell to Earth with a cakra, a lotus bloom, a club, and a conch shell in his four arms. (This might be a reference to a cakra as a plate-like weapon.)

The chakras are mentioned as mystics concentrating on consciousness in the Yoga Upanishads (about 600 B.C.) and subsequently in Patanjali's Yoga Sutras (approximately 200 B.C.). Most translations of Patanjali read a dualism between Purusha (pure awareness) and Prakriti (the prima material of the world), implying that the goal of yoga was to transcend nature in order to recognize pure cognizance free of the vacillations of the psyche and feelings.

However, the term yoga implies a burden or association, so this acknowledgment of awareness should eventually reintegrate with nature for a higher amalgamation.

During the second half of the first thousand years, BC, the chakra framework and Kundalini yoga emerged within the Tantric tradition. Tantra means "device for extending" (tra) and may be thought of as a loom on which the texture of nature is woven from the connection of opposing energy. Tantra is often regarded as a sexual norm in the West. However, sacred sexuality is only a small part of a larger theory that includes numerous acts of yoga, devotion to divinities, particularly Hindu goddesses, and a synthesis of the innumerable pyloric powers known to humanity.

The main lesson regarding chakras that has come to us in the West is an interpretation by the Englishman, Arthur Avalon, in his 1919 book, The Serpent Power. The Sat-Cakra-Nirupama, written by an Indian scholar in 1577, and the Padaka-Pancaka, published in the ninth century, both include depictions of the focuses and associated rituals. Another tenth-century material, known as the Gorakshashatakam, provides instructions for chakra reflection. These works form the foundation of our current understanding of the chakra concept and Kundalini yoga.

There are seven important chakras in these norms, and they all reside within the human body, above the physical body.

We may understand from modern physiology that these seven chakras correspond to the seven basic nerve ganglia that emanate from the spinal segment. There are smaller chakras mentioned in ancient scriptures, such as the soma chakra, which is located just above the third eye, and the Anandakanda lotus, which holds the Celestial Wishing Tree (Kalpataru) of the Heart Chakra, as well as minor sub-levels to the main chakras.

In recent years, the concept of chakras, or hidden energy groups inside the body, has captured the Western creative imagination more than for all intents and purposes and has served as the foundation for some other Yoga instruction. However, as with most other ideas derived from Sanskrit sources, the West (despite a slew of researchers) has completely failed to comprehend what the chakra idea meant in its specific context and how one should practice with them.

This article attempts to ameliorate the situation in some way. If you don't have time, you may skip the logical comments I'm about to make and go straight to the rundown of the six key facts concerning chakras that even expert yogis don't understand.

Most critically, how do we define 'chakra'? Chakras (Skt. chakra) are significant foci for contemplation within the human body in Tantric traditions and are considered constructions of vitality appearing like rings or blooms at the points where numerous ns (channels or meridians) unite. They have used structures that are phenomenological in nature because they will, in general, be found where individuals feel passionate or possibly otherworldly energy, and because they have envisaged visionary experiences encountered by persons who meditate.

(As already said, the West has so far failed to grasp chakras. Let me clarify that by 'the West,' I mean Euro-American culture as well as portions of contemporary Indian culture that are schooled by the Euro-American social grid. Since it is nearly impossible to find a type of yoga in India that is not influenced by Euro-American ideas about it when I use the term 'Western' I also recall the vast majority of yoga lessons in India today that are available in English)

Okay, I'll tell you straight: Western yoga sees nothing significant about the chakras that the first custom thought was significant about them. If you read a book like Anodea Judith's popular Wheels of Life or something similar, understand that you are not reading a work of yoga reasoning, but rather of Western otherworldliness, because of three primary sources:

1. Previous works of Western mystery that use and modify Sanskrit terminology without properly understanding them (such as Theosophist C.W. Leadbeater's The Chakras, 1927).
2. John Woodroffe's erroneous 1918 reading of a book on the chakras authored in Sanskrit in 1577 (see below for more on this).
3. Books written in the twentieth century by Indian yoga gurus who, for the most part, rely on sources 1) and 2). So far, only books on the chakras based on sound cognizance of the first Sanskrit sources exist in the literary world.

'However, does that make a difference?' yogis inquire. 'I've gained so much from Anodea Judith's book and others like it; don't take it away from me!' I can't and won't. Whatever advantage you've obtained, from whatever source, is genuine if you state it is. I'm only here to tell you two things: first, when current Western writers on the chakras claim to be introducing old lessons, they're deceiving you—yet they have no idea because they can't assess the legitimacy of their source materials (because they don't understand Sanskrit). Second, for those who are interested, I'm here to explain to you a little bit about what yogic notions imply in their specific context (because I'm a Sanskrit scholar and specialist who tends to lean toward traditional structures). Nobody except you can determine whether or not something is advantageous to you. I'm not claiming that more experience is always better. I'm trying not to imply that the Western enigma has no supernatural motivation. I'm only attempting to approximate the historical reality in plain English phrases. So, I'll go ahead and do it now: the six essential realities regarding the chakras that cutting-edge yogis don't have the foggiest notion.

1. THERE IS NOT JUST ONE CHAKRA SYSTEM IN THE ORIGINAL TRADITION, BUT MANY.

What a large number! The theory of the unobtrusive body and its energy points called chakras (or padmas (lotuses), ādhāras, lakṣyas (center foci), and so on) derives from Tantric Yoga, which flourished from 600-1300 CE and is still active today. Tantric Yoga was developed (about the year 900 or so) with all of the many components of the custom verbalized chakra framework and a few branches stated several times. Depending on the content and ancestry, five-chakra frameworks, six-chakra frameworks, seven, nine, ten, twelve, twenty-one, and more chakras are advised. The seven- (or, in reality, six and one) chakra framework that Western yogis believe in is simply one of several, and it became popular about the fourteenth century (see point #4 below).

Now I understand what you're thinking: 'However, which framework is correct? 'How many chakras are there in total?' That brings us to our first major misunderstanding. The chakras do not care for organs in the physical body; they are not permanent entities that can be studied in the same way that professionals examine neurological ganglia (with which the chakras were confused in the eighteenth century). The vitality body (skshma-sharra) is a very liquid reality, as one would anticipate from something nonphysical and hypersensual. The vitality, body may experiment with any number of vitalities focuses, depending on the person and the yoga practice being performed.

There are a couple of focal points that are found in all frameworks: explicitly, in the lower gut or sexual center, in the heart, and in or near the crown of the head because these are three places in the body where people all over the world experience both passionate and profound marvels. However, aside from those three, the chakra frameworks found in the first writing have a wide range of variations. Except in comparison with a specific practice, one is not increasingly 'right' than another. For example, if you're practicing a five-component practice, you'll need a five-chakra framework (see point #6 below). A six-chakra structure is used to conceal the life of six separate divinities. Isn't that obvious? Regardless, this critical piece of information has yet to reach Western yoga.

We've only just started down this hare opening, Alice. Do you want to find out more?

    2. THE CHAKRA SYSTEMS ARE PRESCRIPTIVE INSTEAD OF DESCRIPTIVE.

This is maybe the most important aspect. In general, English publications will depict the chakra framework as an existential reality, using simple terminology (such as "the Andhra chakra is at the base of the spine and it is red, etc.). In any case, in a large portion of the first Sanskrit sources, we are not being instructed about the status quo; rather, we are being instructed about a specific yogic practice: we are to imagine an unpretentious item made of colored light, shaped like a lotus or a turning wheel, at a specific point in the body, and after that enact mantric syllables in it, for a specific reason. Finally, when you understand this, point #1 above bodes well. The books are prescriptive – they tell you what you should do to achieve a certain goal using magical ways. When the exacting Sanskrit reads, in its curved design, 'four-petaled red lotus at the base of the body,' we should comprehend 'The yogi should envision a four-petalmoldeds.' For further information, see item #5 below.

3. THE CHAKRAS' PSYCHOLOGICAL CONDITIONS ARE COMPLETELY MODERN AND WESTERN.

We read on many websites and uncountable publications that the mūlādhāra chakra is associated with endurance and security, that the maṇipūra chakra is associated with resolution and confidence, and so on. The enlightened yogi should recognize that the chakras' link to mental states is an advanced Western development that started with Carl Jung. Perhaps such associations speak to genuine experiential factors for specific individuals (however, not without preparation), but we don't find them in Sanskrit sources. I'm only aware of one specific scenario, which is the 10-chakra framework for yogi-performers, about which I've written a blog post. In any case, we don't find each chakra associated with a specific feeling or mental state in that thirteenth-century framework; rather, every petal of every lotus chakra is associated with an unmistakable sense or mental state, and there is by all accounts no example by which we could make a mark for the chakra all in all.

But wait, there's more. Almost all of Anodea's many connections in The Indian sources provide no foundation for Judith's Wheels of Life. Judith informs us that each chakra is associated with a specific substantial organ, some real breakdowns, specific nourishments, a specific metal, a mineral, an herb, a planet, a method of yoga, a suit of the tarot, a Sephora of Jewish supernatural quality, and a chief heavenly messenger of Christianity! None of these connections are mentioned in the primary sources. Judith or her teachers made them reliant on saw likenesses. This also applies to the essential oils and jewels that various publications and websites claim to compare to each chakra. (It is worth noting that Judith includes data from a distinct Sanskrit source [the Ṣaṭ-cakranirūpaṇa, for which read below] under the mark 'Lotus Symbols' for each chakra.)

When you're suffering confidence difficulties, placing a certain kind of gem on your stomach and seeing it filtering your maṇipūra chakra definitely won't help you feel any better. Perhaps it will, depending on the individual. While this training is unquestionably unconventional and has not been tried overages (which is the true purpose of custom), God knows there's more on paradise and earth than my realist mind desires.

In any event, people, in my opinion, should be aware when the family of training spans a few decades rather than hundreds of years. If training is valued, you don't have to lie about where it came from, right?

Hello, do you like this post? Do you need any other information? Please pursue my email list at that moment! You will not get frequent mailings, and we will never reveal your email address.

4. THE POPULAR SEVEN-CHAKRA SYSTEM COMES NOT FROM ANCIENT SCRIPTURE, BUT FROM A TREATISE WRITTEN IN 1577.

The chakra structure that Western yogis adhere to is contained in a Sanskrit text written by a person called Prananda Yati. He completed his material (the

Ṣaṭ-chakra-nirūpaṇa or 'Clarification of the Six Chakras,' which is part six of a larger work) in 1577, and it was translated into English exactly 100 years later, in 1918.

This seven-chakra structure was described as "late and to some extent atypical" in an earlier version of this text. However, after a few days, I realized that I was confused. In essence, the rad-tilaka is a thirteenth-century post-textual material that has a simplified rendering of a comparable seven-chakra structure.

However, that content acknowledges the existence of various chakra frameworks (for example, 12 or 16 chakra frameworks). We also find an increasingly elaborate version of a comparable arrangement in the fourteenth or fifteenth-century Śiva-samhitā. Regardless, most yogis (both Indian and Western) are familiar with the seven-chakra framework through Prananda's sixteenth-century work, or through John Woodroffe's somewhat identical and perplexing interpretation of it in 1918. It is sufficient to establish that this seven-chakra structure has dominated for the past four or five centuries. However, the facts confirm that the Westernized seven-chakra framework you are familiar with is based on mid-twentieth-century mediums' understanding of an imperfect interpretation of a non-scriptural source. This in no way, shape, or form refutes it but rather helps to cast doubt on its authority.

5. THE MAIN PURPOSE OF A CHAKRA SYSTEM IS TO SERVE AS A TEMPLATE FOR NYSA, MANTRA INSTALLATION, AND DEITIES.

The primary objective of any chakra framework was unquestionable to serve as a layout for nyāsa, which suggests the creation of mantras and divinity energies for precise purposes of the inconspicuous body. Despite the fact that a great number of people are interested in chakras nowadays, hardly any of them are using them for their intended purpose. That is fine. I'm not here to confuse anybody but rather to educate those who are interested.

The three most notable features of the chakra frameworks in the early sources are:

1) that the supernatural clues of the Sanskrit letter set are spread among the 'petals' of all the chakras in the framework, 2) that each chakra is associated with a distinct Great Element (Earth, Water, Wind, Fire, and Space), and 3) that each chakra is associated with a specific Hindu divine or gods.

This is because, as previously explained, the chakra structure is essentially a nyāsa format. at nyāsa (lit. 'placing,' you imagine a specific mantric syllable at a specific location for a specific chakra in your energy body while silently articulating its sound.

This training is unmistakably installed in a socially specific setting wherein the hints of the Sanskrit language are viewed as particularly amazing vibrations that can frame a compelling piece of an enchanted practice that realizes otherworldly freedom or common advantages through mysterious methods. Conjuring the image and energy of a certain god into a specific chakra is also socially evident. However, if Western yogis come to understand what those gods rely on, the training may be important for them as well, though probably not as much as for someone who grew up with those gods as paradigmatic symbols adorning their intuitive personalities.

Each chakra framework includes the alleged Cause-gods (Karana-devatās). These deities form a stable grouping: from the lowest chakra to the highest, they are Ganesh, Brahm, Vishnu, Rudra, Vara, Sadiva, and Bhairava, with the first and final of these often not appearing, depending on the number of chakras. The final divinity in the Cause-gods list is never a definitive god of the given framework, because that god (whoever it is) is enthroned in the sahasrāra or thousand-petaled lotus on the crown of the head (which isn't a chakra because chakras are penetrated by Kualin in her climb or plunge, whereas the sahasrāra is her final goal and home). In this manner, Bhairava (the most enigmatic version of Shiva) may be recalled for the list of Cause-gods when he is lifted above by the Goddess, the latter being a definite divinity in a huge number of these frameworks.

6. THE SEED MANTRAS YOU BELIEVE GO WITH THE CHAKRAS IN FACT GO

WITH THE ELEMENTS INSTALLED IN THOSE CHAKRAS.

This is less complicated than it seems. You are aware that LAM is the seed-mantra (bīja) of the mūlādhāra chakra. It most emphatically is not. Nowhere in Sanskrit, not even in Prananda's somewhat distorted syncretic record. Furthermore, the mantra of the swādhiṣṭhāna chakra is not VAM. What, pause?

It's simple: LAM (rhymes with 'thumb') is the seed-mantra of the Earth component, which is taught in most chakra awareness exercises in the mūlādhāra. VAM is the seed-mantra of the Water component, which is presented in swādhiṣṭhāna (or, at the very least, in the seven-chakra framework you consider).RAM represents fire, YAM represents wind, and HAM represents space. (All of these bijas rhyme with 'thumb,' but I should point out that in Tantric Yoga, the natural bijas have another vowel sounds that are seen to be much more noteworthy.)

So, the main issue is that the basic mantras related to the first five chakras on every site you can Google don't really have a place with those chakras fundamentally, but rather with the five Elements introduced in them. This is necessary to know if you ever need to add one of those components in a better location. "Pant! "Can I do that?" Indeed, the Elements are introduced in various Tantric ancestors at entirely different points. For example, the Saiddhntika heritage was brought to earth via the heart chakra. What effect can incorporate the Wind component in the heart community have on your connections? (Remember that YAM is the mantra of Air/Wind, not the anāhata chakra, whose natural chant is OM.) Have you ever noticed how cutting-edge American yogis have fragile connections? Could this be related to repeatedly summoning Wind fair and square of the heart?

Nahhh... (I can be hilarious now since just a small portion of my perusers have gotten it this far.) So maybe you could bring some Earth into your heart at some time since establishing is beneficial to your heart. Overall, it's beneficial to remember that LAM is the Earth component mantra, not the mūlādhāra-chakra mantra.

Furthermore, the majority of the geometric figures associated with chakras today are also appropriately associated with the Elements.

Earth is often represented by a (yellow) square, Water by a (shiny) sickle moon, Wind by a hexagram or six-pointed star, Fire by a (red) triangle, and Space by a circle. So, when you see those figures engraved in the outlines of the chakras, you immediately realize that they are depictions of those specific Elements, not of a geometry inherent in the chakra itself.

This brings me to my last point: even a Sanskrit source might be confusing. For example, in Prananda's sixteenth-century teaching, which serves as the foundation for the mainstream contemporary chakra framework, the Five Elements are presented in the first five chakras of a seven-chakra framework. However, this does not always work because, in all traditional frameworks, the Space component is introduced at the crown of the head because that is where the yogī encounters a wide opening into infinite space. Because space is the component that converges into the boundless, it must be at or near the crown. I believe Prananda placed Space at the throat chakra because he lived during a period of increasing overbearing adherence to the received custom without basic reflection (a pattern that has unfortunately continued), and the convention he received was a Kaula one in which the old-style Cause-divinities were pushed down to make way for higher gods (explicitly Bhairava and the Goddess), and the components were uncritically held melded to t (However, the fact that Prananda was relying on Kaula sources isn't obvious, since rather than enthroning the Goddess at the sahasrāra, as one would anticipate in a Kaula seven chakra framework, we find Paramaiva there, maybe because of the influence of Vedānta. For further information, see the comments section's inquiries and responses.)

We've only just begun to explore this topic. No, I'm not kidding.

It's incredibly puzzling, as shown by research into academic writing such as Dory Heilijgers-Seelen's or Gudrun Bühnemann's. It takes incredible perseverance and focuses to attempt to read, much alone make such work. So, here's what I anticipate will happen as a result of this post: Some low lines—a couple of fewer cases to power on extremely convoluted subjects.

Perhaps a couple of fewer yoga instructors attempting to explain the chakras to their understudies. Even with fourteen years of Sanskrit under my belt, I'm daunted by the unpredictability of the early sources.

This is still a relatively undiscovered location. So don't assume you know anything about chakras. Inform your yoga students that each chakra book gives just one possible model.

Nothing stated in English is absolutely definitive for yoga practitioners. So, while you're still learning, why not cherish the yoga convictions you've gained even more? We should admit that we don't completely comprehend these antiquated yoga exercises, but rather than attempting to be an expert on some misrepresented variant of them, you can welcome yourself and your understudies to look all the more obviously, truly, cautiously, and non-critically at their own inward comprehension.

All things considered, everything that every yoga master has ever experienced is also present in you.